MORE THAN
BLENDED LEARNING

Designing world-class learning interventions

By Clive Shepherd

THIS BOOK IS DEDICATED TO HANIF SAZEN, FORMER CEO OF SAFFRON INTERACTIVE, WHO SADLY PASSED AWAY IN 2010. IT WAS HANIF WHO, BACK IN 2005, ORIGINALLY SUGGESTED THAT I WROTE THE BLENDED LEARNING COOKBOOK.THIS REPRESENTED THE STARTING POINT OF MY EXPLORATION INTO THE WORLD OF BLENDED LEARNING, WHICH CULMINATES TEN YEARS LATER WITH SOMETHING 'MORE THAN'.

First published by The More Than Blended Learning Company in 2015.

ISBN: 978-1-326-24068-4

www.morethanblended.com

CON-
TENTS

CONTENTS

The concept of blended learning will already be familiar to many of you. After all, people have been blending learning methods and media for as long as there have been things that people need to learn and others willing to teach them. Yet somehow, it is only in the

from webinars to videos, as well as social and collaborative learning, the use of performance support materials and providing opportunities for accelerated on-job learning.

Employers recognise that learning at work takes place continuously,

PREFACE

last ten years that the modern learning professional has fully come to terms with the fact that a single approach – a classroom event, perhaps, a self-study module, or a period of on-job instruction – when used on its own, is unlikely to meet a learning requirement.

Blended learning is right now the strategy of choice for most major employers and for many educational institutions, whether or not they describe their approach as 'blended learning'. The blended learning of today is broad in scope, extending well beyond formal courses to include all sorts of online business communications,

whether or not it is formally planned. They understand that courses are not enough to change behaviour and increase performance. As a result, they increasingly expect more far-reaching solutions that go well beyond the presentation of information and half-hearted attempts at providing opportunities for practice. They want learning solutions that deliver and that places fresh demands on the designers of those solutions.

HOW THIS BOOK CAME ABOUT

This book is for anyone who designs learning interventions for adults and who wants to deliver greater value to the organisations that they serve.

It represents the end product of ten years of thinking about and experimenting with blended solutions for adult learning. At first I thought it should be relatively simple to decide how to combine face-to-face and online approaches to learning. Very quickly I realised that to do a proper job of blending learning you have to solve a whole set of sophisticated problems.

Even the simplest decisions seemed to me, on closer investigation, to be multi-faceted. OK, so let's say you want to replace part of a predominantly classroom curriculum with an element of self-paced e-learning. On the surface this seems like a simple issue of media selection – deciding which of those elements that were previously face to face should in future be delivered online. But hold on! The chances are that, by switching some face-to-face elements to self-study, you are also going to change who it is that the learner learns with (what was previously a group experience is now self-study), the mode of communication (what was

live is now carried out at a time that suits the learner), and often also the underlying learning strategy. All of these decision points need to be carefully and separately considered, not bundled together.

It also became more and more evident to me that formal interventions, however well designed, were rarely enough to satisfy the needs of employers or the goals of learners. Formal input is, in many cases, a necessary ingredient, but it is unlikely to be sufficient. Rather than events alone we need end-to-end processes.

Evidence for this comes from the Corporate Leadership's 2011 survey of 350 line managers in 51 countries[1]. Some 86% of respondents thought that employee learning and development (L&D) was vitally important. Most were supportive of individual events organised by L&D, yet 76% felt that L&D was ineffective or extremely ineffective at supporting their business outcomes. The formal input that L&D was providing was popular but it simply was not delivering in terms of changed behaviour and, ultimately, business performance.

1_ *Thanks to Charles Jennings for drawing this to my attention.*

WHAT THIS BOOK DOES AND DOES NOT ATTEMPT TO DO

A blended solution differs from a conventional intervention in that it contains highly contrasting methods and media. It does this in order to improve both the efficiency (cost, time commitment, flexibility and scalability) and the effectiveness of the solution. Blends are more efficient because they do not focus on a single delivery channel (such as the bricks-and-mortar classroom) when more flexible approaches (such as online media) can do an equally successful job, for at least some of the elements in the solution. Technology is an important enabler here, providing opportunities that we could have only dreamed about 20 years ago. Blends, at least those that employ the *more than* approach, are also more effective, because they emphasise practical application and follow-through.

A blended solution differs from a conventional intervention in that it contains highly contrasting methods and media.

However, this book, as the title implies, is about more than blended learning. It recommends an approach that can be applied to any situation in which there is a requirement to support a population on their learning journey and, as a result, meet a need. You do not have to start out with the intention of devising a blend and, who knows, you may decide on a solution that does not contain highly contrasting methods or media. However, to fulfil the requirement for really effective, end-to-end solutions, you are often likely to end up with a blend, however simple.

Most learning professionals will probably use the *more than* approach to design programmes that have, at their heart, formal elements, such as workshops, instructional materials and assessments. But the approach will work just as well when the primary input comes from, say, the meetings of an action learning set or a series of coaching sessions. It will work whether the programme you have in mind is learner-driven (pulled) or institutionally-driven (pushed). All you need is a learning goal and a conscious attempt to achieve that goal.

So what falls outside the scope of this book? Well, the more than approach will make little sense if you are not making a deliberate attempt to achieve an explicit learning goal. Accidental and incidental learning is important but, by definition, it does not need designing. So you will not apply the more than approach to experiential learning – simply doing the job and reflecting on your experience – although experiential learning may play a part in a blended solution. Similarly, programmes that focus entirely on providing performance support (on-demand access to information and tools) or on establishing communities of practice (COP) would both be out of scope, even though performance support and COPs could form a part of many blends[2].

The *more than* approach helps you to establish a top-level design for a learning intervention in terms of its overall structure and strategy. It may also provide you with inspiration when it comes to the detailed design, development and deployment of the particular building blocks within your blend (such as classroom workshops, social learning activities or digital learning materials), but these are not the focus of this book and you will have to look elsewhere for detailed guidance[3].

2_ If you are interested in the wider, strategic issues involved in organisational learning, covering all the contexts from experiential to on-demand, non-formal to formal, then see my book The New Learning Architect.

3_ I have been involved in a number of books designed to help you design, develop and deliver the various elements in a blend: Live Online Learning: A Facilitator's Guide introduces you to the joys of the virtual classroom; Digital Learning Content: A Designer's Guide provides comprehensive guidance with regard to the development of online content.

YOU CAN USE THIS BOOK IN A NUMBER OF WAYS.

Part 1 provides an introduction, which you will find particularly useful if you need to understand the rationale behind the *more than* approach. Part 2 summarises the approach in a single chapter – good for an overview or a refresher. Parts 3–7 go through each aspect of the approach in a lot more detail, including all sorts of useful reference material. And along the way you can gain inspiration from case studies of successful blended solutions across a wide range of organisations.

You'll discover what *more than blended learning* really means:

* *More than* a classroom sandwich (you don't need a book to explain how to create a solution based on a classroom course sandwiched between pre- and post-activities).

* *More than* one way to blend (not just a mix of face-to-face and online).

* *More than* courses (this approach will work just as well with interventions that focus on less formal ways of learning).

* *More than* a process for designing blends (we believe this is a universal design process that you can apply every day).

And finally, *More than blended learning* is more than a book. It is, in itself, a blend of offerings including video case studies, tools and templates, explainer videos and interactive materials. Please do take a moment to explore these resources at www.morethanblended.com.

PART 1
INTRODUCTION

STRICTLY FOR BEGINNERS

It was after another long trip away for Harry Keane, this time to Hong Kong, to chair a conference and run a workshop. When he puts these assignments in the diary he does so with enthusiasm, because they provide an opportunity to go somewhere new and meet some interesting people. When it comes to it,

The implication for those left at home is rather different – none of the jet lag and the hours spent cramped up on a plane, but also none of the excitement. This always makes Harry feel a little guilty and, on getting home, he would certainly be reluctant to launch straight away into his own hobbies – playing golf, watching the football and making music.

he still remembered when the very idea of ballroom dancing was a bit of a joke, something that people like him would never dream of doing.

Anyway, they made an appointment at the local dance school and had a chat with one of the teachers. She asked what experience they had (Rita loved dancing, Harry didn't, but neither of

the actuality is several days of travel in each direction, disrupted sleep and a whole week written off. Nowadays Harry also adds on a few days for sightseeing, because otherwise all he experiences is an airport, a motorway and a hotel – he have those in the UK.

So, when Harry's wife, Rita, suggested they take up a new activity that they could do together, he was in a position of weakness and couldn't really refuse. Ballroom dancing was the suggestion. This would not have been Harry's first choice – his experience of dancing was limited to occasional drunken moments, and in spite of the fact that they both followed Strictly Come Dancing avidly,

them had ever tried ballroom) and what they were looking to achieve. They agreed that the two of them would enrol on a series of ten beginners' classes, starting in a couple of weeks. The teacher gave them some material to read beforehand, explaining how the course would work and pointing them to some web sites that would give them a background to the different dances.

The classes themselves were a lot of fun – one hour per week, most of which was spent on the dance floor having a go. Of course the teacher did provide

them with some simple instructions and demonstrated the various steps and moves, but never overloaded them with too much at a time. They soon lost any self-consciousness they might have had (especially Harry) and made quicker progress than they would have thought possible.

A nice touch from the dance school was that they had prepared a series of simple instructional videos that they made available on YouTube for Harry and Rita to watch between classes and practise with at home. This meant that the classes themselves could be as

practical as possible, giving the teacher the opportunity to watch their progress and provide them with feedback.

After the ten weeks were up they had covered all the basics and developed enough confidence to feel that they could progress largely on their own. The dancing still did not come completely naturally, but these were early days and they were on their way.

They took every opportunity to flaunt

their new skills, even entering a few beginners' competitions. They started to work on the fine points of technique and soon realised they needed some help if they were to keep improving. So, they organised occasional coaching sessions with the dance teacher and she helped them to set goals for their performance

which they would review at the next session.

Harry and Rita had made a lot of friends through the classes and met many more as they continued to participate in as many events as they could. They kept in touch with these friends through Facebook and shared their experiences, good and bad. This soon led to much wider networking across the Internet with aspiring dancers like themselves from around the world. These were still early days in their learning journey, but at least they weren't travelling alone.

(c) Wiki Commons

THE SKILLS JOURNEY

Edith Piaf (1915–1963) was a singer of *chanson* and ballads, and one of France's greatest international stars. Her music was often autobiographical, telling of love, loss and sorrow. Perhaps Piaf's most famous song was *Non, je ne regrette rien* – No, I have no regrets.

So what does Edith Piaf have to do with blended learning? Well, to be honest very little. It is just that her name is the perfect way to remember the four phases in an effective blended solution: Preparation, Input, Application, Follow-up. No regrets learning.

The purpose of the **Preparation** phase is to align the learner with the intervention, so both are prepared to receive each other.

The **Input** phase acts as a catalyst for action. It's usually the most formal part of the blend.

In the **Application** phase, the learner applies what they have learned to real-life tasks (or, where this is not possible, to highly authentic tasks).

The **Follow-up** phase is actually the longest. The aim here is to embed the learning into everyday behaviour.

PIAF IN ACTION

Perhaps the best way to explain PIAF is to demonstrate it in action and what better way to do that than with our ballroom dancing story – *Strictly for beginners?*

Preparation	Input	Application	Follow-up
Discussion with dance teacher	Group classes, mainly practical	Lots of practice at home	Individual coaching
Reviewing information about the course	Videos to watch independently		Dancing for fun and competitively
Background reading			Sharing experiences with other dancers

Preparation: This phase started with a discussion at the dance school, which made it possible for the teacher to determine goals, assess prior knowledge and suggest the most suitable course. Harry and Rita were then able to get ready for the start of the course by doing a little background reading.

Input: This phase had two elements – the group classes and the videos that they watched at home. The classes provided the opportunity for supervised practice with expert feedback. The videos delivered some formal input that they could access at our own pace.

Application: This phase consisted of lots of practice carried out at home between the weekly classes. Notice how the Input and Application phases looped, which is often the case with lengthier solutions. The alternative would have been to have had all the classes running back to back, which wouldn't work for obvious reasons – the process would have been physically and psychologically exhausting!

Follow-up: In this phase, the emphasis shifts to one of on-going development of the skills. The obvious way to achieve this is by getting as much practice as possible, which Harry and Rita achieved by taking every opportunity to dance both for fun and in competition. The coaching enabled them to address any gaps that became evident as they benchmarked their skills against others. And by sharing their experiences with other dancers they picked up additional tips and gave each other encouragement.

COURSES AND RESOURCES

PIAF can be seen as a mix of 'courses' and 'resources'[4]. I've borrowed this terminology from Nick Shackleton-Jones. Nick distinguishes between the formal nature of *courses*, where the focus, he believes, should be on engaging the learner emotionally with the topic and building their confidence to continue to learn independently, and the on-going provision of *resources*, both human and in the form of content, to support the learner as they continue to learn and apply their new skills.

In all too many learning interventions, the emphasis is placed almost entirely on courses and these courses consist of no more than what we are now calling the Input phase. In our ballroom dancing example, however, the course actually extends over the first three phases, which considerably improves the chances for a successful outcome. The Preparation phase makes sure that the learner is properly geared up for the course and that the course is aligned to the learner's needs. The Application phase ensures that there are plenty of opportunities for the learner to consolidate the skills and build confidence.

But courses are not enough.

There's nothing wrong with courses as such, it's just that we place too much attention on them and not enough on what happens afterwards. By and large, we would do well to teach much less and to provide much more in the way of support as the learner continues their journey. That's why the Follow-up phase in PIAF is so important. It may be only one of four elements, but it is likely to last the longest and have the greatest impact.

A SKILLS JOURNEY

The ballroom dancing story is an example of what we will be calling a 'skills journey'. As we shall see, this is only one of the forms that a blended solution can take, because sometimes the focus is less on skills and more on knowledge and ideas.

A skills journey can be mapped to what is sometimes called the 'four stages of competence'. This process was conceived by Noel Burch in the 1970s, when he was an employee at Gordon Training International. It has frequently been attributed to the psychologist Abraham Maslow, although there is no evidence of this in his major works.

Here are the four stages:

Unconscious incompetence: Ignorance is bliss. Skilled performance looks so easy when applied effortlessly by experts – surely it can't be that hard.

Conscious incompetence: So then you have a go. 'Oh dear, this is much harder than I thought. There's so much to think about at the same time – I don't know whether I'll be able to manage this.' Unfortunately, that is the stage at which many learning interventions finish – the learner is in a worse emotional state than when they started. Ideally the Input phase would not leave the learner in such an uncomfortable position; they should be well on the way to …

Conscious competence: You continue to practise, with lots of constructive feedback. In time you begin to believe you can really do this thing, even if it takes a lot of conscious effort.

4_ *Nick is a psychologist who has held senior positions with a responsibility for learning at the BBC and at BP. He is a leading-edge thinker as well as a practitioner. I recommend his blog, Aconventional, where you will find that he's now not so sure whether we need courses at all.*

Unconscious competence: In time and with enough practice a skill will become unconscious – you will be able to perform it without effort. Eventually you will wonder what the fuss was all about. The task now appears so easy it almost seems intuitive.

An important principle underlying PIAF when applied to a skills journey is that the job is not done until the learner reaches unconscious competence

(and even then, there is always more to learn). The Preparation phase begins the process of making the learner aware of the gap in their competence. The Input and Application phases bridge the gap and build the learner's confidence. The Follow-up phase ensures that the learner is fully supported as they move to that happy state of unconscious competence.

BLENDING BY SOCIAL CONTEXT

One of the ways to conceive of the *more than* approach is that there is more than one way in which blending can take place. In fact, in this book, we will explore four different ways. All of these can be demonstrated in the ballroom dancing example.

The first way that blending can occur is in the 'social context' in which learning takes place. This might sound like quite a theoretical concept but really just means 'who it is, if anyone, that the learner is learning with'. There are four social contexts.

The first of these is **individual** learning, which provides the learner with the greatest flexibility in terms of when and how they learn but little in the way of support. In the ballroom dancing case, several elements of the blend were individual (although, in this case, 'individual' actually meant Harry and Rita together):

* Reviewing information about the course

* Background reading

* Videos to watch independently

* Lots of practice at home

One-to-one learning provides the opportunity for individualised instruction or support. This may be expensive to supply but can be highly valuable. In the dancing example, both the initial discussion with the dance teacher and the individual coaching fall into this category.

The third option is to learn in a small **group** or cohort, which provides the opportunity for shared experiences and mutual support. In our example, the dance classes were clearly like this.

The fourth option is to learn by interacting with a wider **community**, whether that's other employees in the same organisation or all those out there on the Internet. In the example, the community can be regarded as all those other dancers with whom experiences could be shared.

One of the considerations in designing any blend, whether or not it is a skills journey, is to find just the right social contexts for each element in the blend. The most effective blends tend to have an appropriate balance between social contexts, although it is certainly not necessary to employ every social context in every blend.

BLENDING BY LEARNING STRATEGY

A second way in which a solution can be blended is in terms of the strategies that you employ to facilitate learning. In this book we will use a four-way classification of learning strategies that I have based on work by Ruth Clark and Merlin Wittrock[5]:

The first of the strategies is **exposition**, which is simply the one-way delivery of information. In the ballroom dancing case, the literature about the dance classes and the background reading both fall under this category.

The second strategy is **instruction**, which represents a more formal and structured way of building knowledge or skills. In the case, there are three elements that together can be regarded as an instructional approach: the group classes, the videos for watching independently and the practice at home.

5_ I have borrowed heavily over the years from Clark and Wittrock's analysis although, with the number of changes I have made, we probably parted company a while back. I have never seen this model referred to in any of Clark's most popular works – I found it in the catchily titled Training and Retraining: A Handbook for Business, Industry, Government and the Military, edited by Sigmund Tobias and J D Fletcher, published by Macmillan Reference (2000).

The third strategy, **guided discovery**, puts the learner into situations from which insights can occur. There are many ways in which this strategy can be employed, one of the most common of which is coaching. As we saw, coaching played an important role in the Follow-up phase of our dance school example. Coaching differs from instruction in that the coach adopts a more non-directive approach, encouraging the learner to set goals, plan ways of achieving these goals and reflect on their progress.

The final strategy, **exploration**, puts the learner firmly in control of how they access resources (people and information) that might benefit their learning. In the example, this strategy is exemplified by the way in which Harry and Rita shared experiences with other dancers.

Simple, non-blended learning interventions tend to employ a single strategy, but no single strategy is going to work across Preparation, Input, Application and Follow-up. So, as a designer of blended learning experiences, you will be making judgements about which strategies to use for each element in the blend. These judgements will go a long way to determining the success of your solution.

HOW A CORPORATION MIGHT TEACH BALLROOM DANCING

Now this is not really fair, because corporations don't typically have to teach ballroom dancing and, if they did, many of them would, hopefully, suggest an approach that's not so different to the one we have seen above. However, less enlightened corporate learning designers might come up with the following:

Preparation	Input	Application	Follow-up
Joining instructions	Two-day dance workshop (1.5 days of theory, then one practice session per pair while others observe and provide feedback)	Up to the learner	Printed handouts for reference

I suppose this could be regarded as a blend. Yes, there is some exposition (the joining instructions), some instruction (the workshop) and some exploration (the handouts). In terms of social contexts, the predominant approach is group work, although there's a little bit of individual activity before and after the workshop.

However, this is no more than token blending. As I'm sure you'd agree, the balance is all wrong. There's too much theory and not enough practice (the most typical problem with skills training); there's too much emphasis on the course and not enough on resources; and, as a result, the learner is unlikely to go beyond conscious incompetence.

AND IT ALL LOOKED SO SIMPLE

The ballroom dancing example is a simple enough blend and that has to be a positive thing. However, we have analysed it a number of ways, in terms of courses and resources, stages in developing competence, social contexts and strategies for learning. It might be beginning to look not so simple after all.

But, as a reader of this book, you are on your own skills journey. It could be you're just beginning to feel a little conscious incompetence. Do not be discouraged. All of the concepts that we have discussed in this chapter are easy to understand and apply given some patience and plenty of practice. It is only a matter of time before designing great blends will seem to be an intuitive skill. And your learners will thank you for making the effort.

THE IDEAS ADVENTURE

Not every blended solution addresses a skills gap. Often the intention of the blend is to put across some 'big ideas' that you hope will inform people in their decision-making.

Many interventions are focused on ideas. Take project management for example, or diversity and inclusion, marketing, business studies and aspects of many other jobs, including what we're focusing on here – learning design.

Sometimes we think that topics like this are about knowledge. We believe that if learners know what to do then they will do it. However, life is not so simple. Just because someone tells you that it is a good idea to have a clear objective for a meeting, does not mean that you will make any effort to prepare one. You may have understood the idea intellectually, but you have no emotional commitment to it. Old habits die very hard indeed and, let's face it, we like our habits just as they are.

People don't avoid change as such (after all, we volunteer for some very major changes in our life – new careers, moving house, getting married, having children), but we do resist being

changed. And we regard someone telling us how we should behave differently as just that.

If people are to change, it must be their decision, ideally based on their idea. If we're responsible for making change happen in an organisation (and, as learning professionals, that is our responsibility), then we have to contrive a different type of intervention; one in which learners achieve their own insights into the big ideas that will transform their performance. These interventions have unpredictable outcomes but can lead to remarkable transformations. That's why we call them ideas adventures. There's an element of risk, of course, but then if there was not they wouldn't be adventures.

INTRODUCING THE THREE LS

It's your lucky day. The head of HR has just returned from a Board meeting. She has the brief to put a programme in place that will develop the leadership capabilities of middle managers. Here is how the Board expressed the need:

We want middle managers who are capable of delivering results in a fast-moving business environment; achieved

through cohesive teamwork and the efforts of motivated, high-performing direct reports.

OK, this is the usual, dense corporate jargon but you get the general idea. It's a start but you'll want to follow up by asking a whole load of questions to flesh out the requirement before you get down to any serious design work.

You like to organise your data gathering under three main headings: the learning, the learners and the logistics – more commonly known as the three Ls[6].

The learning: Under this heading you'll collect information on the required learning outcomes. In particular, you'll want to know what type of learning is needed.

The learners: If the learning represents the end point at which you will be aiming, your learners are what you will be starting with. You'll want to know as much as you can about the target population for the intervention.

6_ The three Ls is the brainchild of my colleague, Phil Green. It certainly beats what I started with which was 'learning requirements, audience characteristics, and practical constraints and opportunities'.

The logistics: Finally, you'll want to know what may help you or hinder you as you move your learners towards the learning objectives. How many? By when? For what cost? And so on.

Here is what you managed to find out:

The learning	The learners	The logistics
Insights into the dynamics of effective leadership	Middle managers with 1–20 years of experience	150 managers distributed across a single territory
Increased awareness of own leadership abilities	Responsible for teams of up to 10 direct reports	Aim to complete the formal element of the programme in 24 months
Skills in interacting with individuals and groups in a wide variety of leadership situations	Highly variable leadership awareness and ability	Senior management commitment to the programme includes 'as much time and money as is necessary to do the job properly'.
Confidence to apply new leadership thinking to their work	A minority will have had leadership training before	
	Variable levels of motivation both for the training and for the job	

Looking at the learning requirement, you recognise that there is an interpersonal skills element, but that the primary aim is to help these middle managers to gain insights into the principles of effective leadership. In other words, this is an ideas adventure.

METHODS AND MEDIA

There are many ways that you could meet this requirement but in the end you have to make a judgement on what you feel will work best for your particular population within the constraints that you face. The table below shows the Preparation phase for your blend. You'll notice that, for each of the four phases, we've made a distinction between the methods you will be using to achieve your objectives and the media you have chosen to deliver those methods.

Methods: Learning methods are the tools we use to facilitate learning. They are what determine whether a solution will be effective and that is why we try to get these right first.

As you can imagine, there are lots of learning methods to choose from. To help in making choices, methods can be categorised in terms of the social contexts and learning strategies that they support, concepts that we introduced in the previous chapter.

Media: Learning media are the means by which we implement our chosen methods. Your choice of media will have a major impact on the efficiency and flexibility of your solution.

Again, there are lots of media to choose from and our choices are constantly growing. To help us decide, we can categorise media in terms of the delivery channels and communication modes that they use. Confused? Don't worry; we are going to address these terms in the next parts of this chapter.

Preparation	Methods	Media
	360 degree survey	Online
	Goal-setting with own manager	However practical
	Some background reading	Print or e-book according to preference
	Making contact with the cohort	Online through the virt ual learning environment (VLE)

In this design for the Preparation phase, you have looked to provide the learner with the following:

- insights into their strengths and areas for development with regard to leadership (360-degree survey);

- commitment to some very definite outcomes, with the full support of their manager (goal setting);

- some familiarity with some of the ideas of leadership, so they can start to consider these before the main part of the course (reading);

- socialisation into the group with which they will be learning (making contact).

These are all elements that will prepare the learner to engage fully with the course and explore possible changes in behaviour.

BLENDING BY DELIVERY CHANNEL

In the previous chapter we saw how it was possible to blend by social context (who participates in the learning activities) and learning strategy (the mechanism by which learning takes place). There is a third way in which you can blend and that's in terms of the delivery channel – the mechanism that you use to engage with the learner:

Face to face: The default channel for formal teaching and training throughout history has been face-to-face communication. This is not always the most flexible or economic option, but there are situations in which this is the only approach that will work.

Offline media: By 'offline media' we are talking of self-study media that you can access without an Internet connection. The most obvious examples from recent history are books, tapes and CDs. These media are all in what seems to be terminal decline, but they have been replaced by media such as e-books and MP3s, which have to be downloaded when you are online, but do not require you to be online when you choose to consume them.

Online media: Obviously the Internet has changed everything, providing endless ways for the learner to find information and collaborate with others. As a delivery channel for learning, it is versatile, cost-effective, accessible and flexible. We will see a lot of learning taking place online (a significant proportion of learning already is, largely informally) but it does not suit every circumstance.

Unmediated: Not all learning takes place in the context of a particular delivery channel. When we think of projects, assignments and simple learning through experience, it does not help

us to associate this with a particular channel – it just happens in whatever way the learner thinks best.

Looking back to the Preparation phase for the leadership programme, you can see that a blend of channels has been used: face to face (for the goal setting, although other channels would work as well), online (the 360-degree survey and the work on the VLE) and offline (the reading). In choosing a channel, what is important is that you achieve the most efficient and flexible way of delivering the chosen methods, without compromising the effectiveness of those methods.

On the other hand, the individual study can be accomplished online, making it easier for the learner to access the materials as and when they want and on whichever device they want.

BLENDING BY MODE OF COMMUNICATION

There is a fourth and last way in which you can blend – the mode of communication:

Same-time (sometimes called synchronous) communication happens in real time. It is perhaps the more emotionally engaging of the two modes, but because all participants have to be available at the same time, it takes more organising and is less flexible.

Own-time (or asynchronous) communication does not require a diary commitment, which provides the learner with more opportunity for reflection.

If we look back to the Input phase of the leadership programme, there is a clear distinction between the workshops, which are same-time, and the individual study, which is own-time. This makes for a good balance of immediacy and reflectiveness.

Below, here's a breakdown of the elements of the Input phase. The emphasis in terms of the workshops is on guided discovery – perhaps the best way of helping learners to gain insights into important ideas. These are conducted face to face because the activities are likely to be lengthy and require intensive collaboration – it is hard to see these being successful in a virtual environment.

Input (loops with Application)	Methods	Media
	Group activities, group discussion	Face-to-face workshops
	Individual reading / viewing	Online articles and videos

Let's move on to the Application phase in which the new ideas are tested against the real world:

Application (loops with Input)	Methods	Media
	Individual and group assignments	Submitted through the VLE
	Review sessions	Online – web conferencing
	Individual reflection	A blog on the VLE

Looking first at the delivery channels, the assignments are unmediated, while the rest of the work is online. Moving on to communication modes, the assignments are likely to be a mix of same-time and own-time elements, whereas the review sessions are clearly same-time and the blog very definitely own-time.

FROM COURSES TO RESOURCES

Let's look now at the final part of your ideas adventure, the Follow-up phase. At this point, the emphasis shifts from courses (push) to resources (pull):

Follow-up	Methods	Media
	360-degree survey	Online
	Review session(s) with own manager	However practical
	Final assessment on the basis of demonstrated competence	Submitted online

Notice how assessment is based on demonstrated competence, not knowledge. This is a natural consequence of the PIAF approach, an end-to-end process that starts with a business need and ends only when that need has been met. Contrast this with an approach that focuses mainly on learning outputs.

THE PATH TO
KNOWLEDGE

So far, we have addressed how blended solutions can be constructed to develop skills and to help learners gain insights into big ideas. You might be wondering how knowledge fits into the mix.

Well, at least in a vocational context, knowledge is not usually the end goal of an intervention. Employers do not measure their success in terms of the amount of knowledge achieved by their employees, but in the impact that employees make on their key performance indicators (KPIs).

Knowledge may underpin competent behaviour, but it is performance that matters, however this is achieved.

Having said all this, there will be occasions when you are required to put together an intervention that has the specific aim of providing underpinning knowledge, rather than directly modifying behaviour. Here are some examples:

- Induction to a new organisation (rather than the specific job training that is likely to follow this).

- Briefings on new developments in a particular knowledge domain, e.g. law, medicine, accountancy, academia.

- Providing an understanding of scientific, mathematical and other technical principles and processes as a general background to the work someone does. An example might be explaining how a new engine works to maintenance engineers.

- Providing a briefing on a new product.

- Satisfying an internal verifier or an external regulator for the purpose of periodic compliance testing (although there will sometimes be an even more important need to sell in a big idea, such as the benefits of diversity or the need for security).

Let's take an example and see how it can be mapped to our friend PIAF.

WELCOME TO YOUR NEW JOB

To start a new job is a stressful experience, regardless of how confident you are or experienced in working in similar positions. There is so much to know just to get through your first day. You are under pressure to build a new network of contacts and to prove yourself to your manager and your colleagues.

For the purposes of our example, the need is for a corporate induction programme for new employees joining at the head office of a large organisation. This programme is intended to provide a welcome to the organisation as a whole, not specific job training. Success will be measured by the speed with which new employees are able to settle in and their overall level of satisfaction with their choice of new employer. This is about hopes and fears, not just knowing what to do.

Here is a summary of what we know about the requirement:

The learning	The learners	The logistics
Knowledge of the organisation's history, structure, products and services.	All levels up to and including middle management.	Between 10 and 30 new employees join each month, normally on the first Monday.
Insights into the organisation's values and ways of working.	All ages. Some will have previous experience with a similar employer. For some this will be their first job.	Managers are keen to integrate their departmental inductions and job training with the corporate induction.
Essential knowledge to ensure safety and security from day 1.	Some will be full of confidence, others very apprehensive.	The new induction needs to be up and running in four months.
Essential knowledge about employment policies and benefits.	All will be keen to make a good impression and do well in their new jobs.	There is a budget of £100K to finance new content if necessary.
Knowing how to get information and who to ask for help.	All will be IT literate and speak good English, although for some this will be their second language.	New employees will have access to PCs and internet connectivity at their homes and when they arrive.
		There are well-equipped training rooms and trainers available if they are needed.

Looking first at the Learning column, we can see that the emphasis is on providing knowledge. As will often be the case, there are some exceptions:

- Providing insights into the organisation's values is about the big ideas that underpin how the organisation works. These should be addressed using some form of guided discovery.

- Knowing how to get information is likely to involve using the organisation's intranet and other software tools. There is an element of skill in doing this.

Looking at the Learners column, two points stand out:

- The audience for the programme will be diverse.

- These will not be reluctant learners.

The Logistics column tells us that we have few serious constraints on what we can do, other than that we need to get a move on.

A LITTLE GAMIFICATION CAN BE A GOOD THING

Preparation	Methods	Media
Before your first day in new job	Interactive multimedia tutorials organised into modules and structured into levels. You advance through the levels by completing knowledge checks. These materials also include interviews with typical staff in a wide variety of positions, talking about what it is like to work in the organisation.	Online
	An essential survival kit of information you need for your first day, including topics such as security and fire safety.	A PDF that you can print out and bring with you or access from your smart phone.
	The learner is allocated a buddy from their new department. This person gets in touch to make sure you are having no difficulty with the tutorials and know where to meet them on the first day.	Telephone

This phase is critical, because it ensures that the learner is able to hit the ground running on their first day, while also hopefully relieving any anxiousness that they might have.

Importantly, the tutorials provide only the absolutely essential information that any new starter would need. It is completely counter-productive to bombard the learner with detail that they could not possibly remember. Not only does overloading the learner not work in terms of learning, it causes unnecessary stress.

They will have many weeks, months and years ahead to develop a more thorough understanding of their new company.

You will have noticed that there is an element of 'gamification' to the way the tutorials are structured. By organising the modules into levels, in a similar way to a video game, the learner is provided with an additional incentive to study. Gamification, which might also include high scores and leaderboards, challenges of increasing difficulty, as well as badges and other rewards, is a useful way to increase engagement in what is typically a tough process of acquiring knowledge.

A word of caution about knowledge checks. While these contribute to the gamification effect, they cannot be relied upon as a formal test of lasting knowledge, simply because they occur too early. As we all know, last-minute study might get us through an exam, but is no guarantee that we will be able to recall this information in the future. Ebbinghaus warned us more than a hundred years ago that the 'forgetting curve' means we forget most of what we learn in a matter of hours. It takes plenty of repetition, rehearsal and practical application to ensure that learning is lasting.

The video interviews are important too, getting beyond the 'corporate gloss' to provide the learner with an insight into real people doing real jobs.

KNOWING WHERE TO FIND INFORMATION IS AS IMPORTANT AS 'WHAT' YOU KNOW

Input	Methods	Media
First thing	Meet your buddy who helps you through building security and takes you to your department.	Face to face
Second thing	Saying hello to your manager and co-workers, and taking a tour of the department and the nearby facilities.	Face to face
Ideally in the first two days	A welcome session for all of the latest joiners. An opportunity to follow-up on the pre-study and to answer any questions.	Classroom
In the same session	Some guided discovery exercises to bring out the organisation's values: tell a story and then ask 'What would we do in that situation?' Follow up with discussion and some video 'vox pops' from current staff explaining what they do and why.	Classroom
In the same session	A 'treasure hunt' activity in groups to search out information on the organisation's intranet. Followed up with a demo of the intranet.	Classroom

On your first day in a new job you want as much face-to-face contact with your new colleagues as possible. Survival depends on building a new network, so this process should start straight away. Clearly the most important people you need to meet are your manager and colleagues, but there also advantages to be gained by meeting up with others who, like you, are new to the organisation.

Notice that the welcome session is not an 'information dump' – the essential information was provided in the Preparation phase and the detail will follow later. When you're a novice, you will not be able to cope with too much information at one time and will, anyway, be more focused on what it takes to do your job than on the mechanics of the organisation as a whole.

You might think that learning about the organisation's intranet is a low priority but, assuming this is up-to-date and comprehensively stocked with useful information, it could be a life-saver. If you know your way around the intranet, you become much less of a drain on your colleagues.

THE IMPORTANCE OF THE BUDDY

Application	Methods	Media
In the coming week or two	Your buddy checks you are OK on a regular basis, helps you to obtain answers to your questions and makes sure you continue to build your network.	Face to face

The Application phase may not have as much significance along a path to knowledge as it would do with a Skills Journey or an Ideas Adventure, but still deserves thought. What you are talking about here is a gradual removing of the scaffolding from a situation in which the learner is a novice in the particular subject area, to one in which they can independently take responsibility for acquiring additional knowledge.

Buddies are a big part of this design and their competence should not be a matter of chance. They would need special training to make sure they were sufficiently knowledgeable and confident in interacting with new starters.

COURSES AND RESOURCES REVISITED

Follow-up	Methods	Media
	An official sign-off from your buddy and a review of how the induction programme has gone.	Face to face
	Access to reference information as and when you need it.	Online
	Continuous acquisition of 'tacit knowledge' through interaction with others and job experience.	All
	Additional formal training where necessary to cover any essential regulatory and mandatory topics.	Online

In the chapter on the Skills Journey, we introduced the concept of 'courses and resources' and explained how important it was that more emphasis be placed on the latter. There are several reasons for this:

- Recent findings[7] from cognitive neuroscience have made us much more aware of just how difficult it is to acquire new knowledge, particularly when this is 'semantic' – factual and conceptual. As a result, we should try to minimise the load we place on learners in terms of required knowledge.

- In many jobs there is now too much for any person to know and this information is getting out of date quickly. It is a hopeless task to 'teach' this information – far better to refer to it as and when it is needed.

- It has never been easier to make information available on demand with the near ubiquity of access to the Internet and the 24/7 availability of mobile devices. Online information has become, for many of us, our 'outboard brain' – an extension of our memory.

7_ A useful and accessible primer would be Brain Rules by Dr John Medina, Pear Press (2009).

• Those who make frequent use of online information no longer see the necessity of 'knowing lots of stuff'. They will complain (and rightly so) if they are asked to memorise more than is absolutely necessary.

Of course some knowledge is essential to any job – without it we would have no credibility with those with whom we interact and would find it hard to react quickly to situations as they arise. One of the most important tasks for designers of blended solutions is to separate what really must be learned from what can be safely accessed on demand. They must also resist the pressure from subject experts who would have you believe that every aspect of their discipline is essential.

Contrary to what may have been thought in the past, accessing information as and when you need it does not make you any less of a professional. Lawyers, surgeons, airline pilots, software engineers, even designers of learning interventions, rely on reference materials to tackle those trickier and less common situations that arise from time to time.

NOT ALL KNOWLEDGE CAN EASILY BE MADE EXPLICIT

So far we have focused on *explicit knowledge*, which can be easily articulated and assessed. This can be distinguished from *tacit knowledge*, which is much harder to teach formally. While we all have this knowledge, we are often not aware of what we know or how it can be valuable to others.

Tacit knowledge explains 'how things work around here' – those hundreds, if not thousands, of cause and effect relationships (usefully described as 'principles') which allow us to solve problems, make decisions and otherwise make sense of things. The more you know about a subject, whether that's your technical discipline, a hobby or the way to interact with others, the richer becomes your network of associations – what psychologists call *schemas*.

Novices have schemas with very few connections. Because new knowledge – explicit or tacit – has to be connected to what is already there, they struggle to cope with large volumes of information. They don't know what they don't know; they cannot distinguish between information that is important and information that can be safely ignored.

The effective transfer of tacit knowledge generally requires prolonged experience and extensive personal contact. While tacit knowledge can be acquired as a result of courses, it will most often occur through serendipitous contact with other learners, rather than formal teaching. This explains why the Follow-up phase is so valuable and why it pays to be proactive in helping learners to establish the social networks that will allow tacit knowledge to be shared.

WHY *MORE THAN* BLENDED LEARNING?

At this point, you may be asking in what sense the process that I have been describing is 'more than' blended learning. As you have made the effort to get this far, it is only fair that I explain.

MORE THAN A CLASSROOM SANDWICH

First of all, the blends described in this book are more than a simple mix of classroom and e-learning, where the primary intention is to reduce classroom days and thereby save costs. There is nothing inherently wrong with the idea of mixing classroom sessions with pre- and/or post-e-learning, in those situations where this clearly does the job, and without sacrificing quality. But there are so many other ingredients that we could put in the mix and we don't want to overlook the opportunities that these provide.

And too often blending is seen as a trade-off between quality and quantity – we give up a little of the effectiveness of our all-classroom experience in order to gain some cost savings and flexibilities. The approach described in this book does not work that way: effectiveness is a constant, a given; efficiency is something to strive for, but not at the expense of an intervention that works.

MORE THAN ONE WAY TO BLEND

The most common description of blended learning is as a combination of face-to-face and online learning – in other words a blend of what we have been calling delivery channels.

This is helpful up to a point but not enough to explain what it is that makes blending work. Let's return to that combination of the face-to-face classroom and some self-study e-learning. Yes, you are combining delivery channels, but the most significant aspect of the blend from the learner's perspective is likely to be the combination of two very different social contexts – learning with a group of peers and learning alone.

This same example also mixes communication modes, because the classroom is same-time and the e-learning is own-time. And who knows, it's possible that different strategies will be used for each element as well.

There is more than one way to blend. We have looked at social contexts, strategies, delivery channels and communication modes. All of these need to be aligned to the particular learning requirements, learner characteristics and logistical constraints. And all need to be in balance.

You do not need to blend in all four ways to be effective and efficient. It is, for example, perfectly possible to design a great blend that takes place entirely online. What is important is that all these issues are carefully assessed and the right judgements made for the particular situation. That's more than we are probably used to doing.

MORE THAN COURSES

Blends that focus entirely on formal elements, typically courses of some form or another, may be successful in moving the learner along their learning journey but often do not go far enough to satisfy the original need. This need is rarely for learning in itself, but for the improvements in task performance to which learning can contribute.

The process described in this book is end-to-end – from the manifestation of the need to its eventual satisfaction. It is unlikely that this happy process will be reached without application to the real world and then on-going refinement thereafter, which requires resources – both people and content – rather than courses.

The Preparation–Input–Application–Follow-up (PIAF) process that we advocate places as much emphasis on resources as it does on courses, perhaps even more. To some extent learners will make this happen for themselves – when they detect a gap they will make their own efforts to close it. But PIAF does not leave this to chance; it predicts what resources will be needed and puts these in place, providing learners with the support they need until they are fully independent.

MORE THAN A PROCESS FOR DESIGNING BLENDS

There is nothing in the process described in this book that is specific to blended solutions. You could go through a similar series of steps to design any learning intervention and you would find the structure useful.

On the other hand, it is hard to envisage an end-to-end, PIAF solution that could be accomplished using a single approach – a single delivery channel, single communication mode, single social context and single strategy. In fact it is probably impossible.

There is no need to use distinct design processes for blended and non-blended solutions. We believe that the *more than* approach is a universal design process that you can apply every day. Go give it a try.

THE

BL

COLLECTION:

VODAFONE

MARKETING CAPABILITY

This solution works for a demanding global audience of marketing professionals for which previous attempts have fallen flat. It achieves this by condensing the theoretical component to a level at which it can be summarised in just three slides, and then focusing in on the practical ways in which a unified approach to marketing can be applied across a major corporation.

TALKING ABOUT MARKETING CAPABILITY

Mohsin, *Ghafoor*, Group Commercial Learning Lead, Vodafone

Vodafone, as you probably know, is a global telecommunications provider, now operating fixed line and mobile services. We operate in over 20 countries and have over 450 million customers worldwide, with partner agreements in more than 70 countries globally.

My role at Vodafone is to lead the commercial learning and development function, and a significant part of that role has been to develop our marketing capability globally.

There are four main reasons why we considered this to be important. The first is really about our growth as an organisation, how we make connections with our customers and how we offer our global customers products and services that they really need and want. So this is very much about driving our growth in a market in which competition is ever increasing and in which the situation has changed dramatically over the last ten to fifteen years.

The second reason is to make sure that we sign up to one way of marketing. We don't want twenty different ways of developing an insight or a proposition, or thinking about commercial strategy. For efficiency and best practice, we want Vodafone to sign up to *one way* that every marketer in the company understands and delivers on a daily basis.

Thirdly, I think it's important to say that we want Vodafone to be a hothouse for marketing talent. We want the best talent out there in the marketplace. We want the best graduates from universities, saying that they want to join Vodafone to develop a fantastic marketing career.

And finally, we want to be ready for the future because the market will get even more competitive and we want our marketers to be ready for that and deliver best quality and fantastic solutions for our customers.

I want to outline some of the context I found when I came into the role. There had been several attempts at Vodafone to deliver a marketing academy and for one reason or another they had never landed, so it was very important for me to understand why that was, talk to people throughout the business, spend the time with some of our marketing leaders across markets and work out what it is that's really going to make a difference. Given that our marketers are spread over 20 markets, it's very difficult to be all things to all people but we needed to know what would give us the best chance of pleasing the majority.

I think a few points came out from that research. One was that I wanted the content and the learning experience to be very practical and not an exercise in theory; something that our marketers could take away and start using immediately – tools, templates and ideas that could be applied to real business problems.

The second element I wanted to highlight was relevance to the day job. We want our marketers, when they experience the learning, to instantly think, 'Ah, I see how that resonates; I see how that could work in what I do, day in, day out.'

And the third element was to make it a fun experience. I've had an interesting time meeting many marketers over the last two years and I would say they are a certain type. They want a fantastic experience, they want things to look good, and they want it to be fun and engaging, so that was the brief I gave in terms of what I was trying to achieve with the programme.

The target audience is globally dispersed, which presents a challenge itself in how to deliver the message. They use business English in the working environment but, for a lot of our audience, English is their second language, so we had to make sure that the content was clear, concise and understandable.

Peter Kirkby, Oxford SM

At the heart of the solution is the Vodafone way of marketing that Oxford SM designed so that people can hold the framework very much in their heads. It tries to break down the silos that we'd observed in Vodafone.

Working through with the subject matter experts at Vodafone, we realised we were going to have to find a way of making the learning very tangible and show clearly what the output was that we were looking to achieve. Because we were working with global subject experts, there was also this dynamic of trying to connect global more effectively with local. What we did was summarise the entire Vodafone way of working, from strategy through to execution, on three slides.

Everything we do in the learning drives towards populating something in those three slides.

So that's at the heart. Then there was the e-learning which allowed people to understand specific elements of the Vodafone way of marketing. Beyond that, there's a two-day marketing workshop that allows people to experience the whole Vodafone way of thinking about marketing in a very rich, immersive face-to-face environment. There's a competitive case study that runs all the way through, and at the end of the two days the teams present their cases back to senior management.

Our challenge then was, how do you make sure that senior management and leaders in the business understand the core elements of the Vodafone way of marketing? Rather than make them go through the two days, what we did was leave all the stimulus in the room and have them come back for the third morning, review the stimulus and decide for themselves what great looks like – what makes some of the examples stand out as better than others.

After that, we help them to develop their own capability roadmap for their organisation – if that's what great looks like, then what steps are you going to take to get there? By this stage they've got the full experience. At the same time they will identify areas where they need to do more – perhaps more detail on insight or more experience on proposition. What we've done is to develop specific workshops around these so that teams and organisations can go deeper into any area where they've identified a specific gap.

Let's take the two-day propositions workshop for example, which we run very differently as a 'hackathon'. We start with two hours of theory but for the rest of the two days they then work in their natural teams to develop a Vodafone solution to a Vodafone business problem, drawing on the experts in the room to help them through that experience. At the end they present back, again to senior management. All of the stimulus and the output from the 'winning' entry goes to the person who looks after that proposition globally in Vodafone. So you get this virtual cycle of learning going, with genuine output that's going to make a commercial difference.

Beyond that, Vodafone have then provided a six-month programme for their high-end managers, that they can do through a leading business school. Again, our material links to that so that even the senior guys are getting a holistic experience.

Mohsin

There were three things that were important to me when considering the design of the portal: it should be easy to use, easy to access and easy to understand. So, not too much text, clearly signposted learning content and the fewest clicks possible to get to what you wanted. I would describe it as elegant simplicity – nice to use, nice to look at and very interactive; lots of video with real marketers talking about their experience with the academy and how they've been able to put it to good use; lots of additional content – informal learning I would call it – including best practice articles and video. One of the aims of the academy was to bring together the best of what's going on outside but also to make marketers realise that we do some great stuff internally.

The e-learning material was developed for us by Lumesse. There were several elements to the e-learning that I thought were important. Firstly there's the design – it was important that it was fun, engaging, and not your standard 'click, click' and 'how soon can I get through this?' It has lots of colour, it's low on text and has video embedded. It's enriched with tools and templates, so very practically focused – definitely not your standard e-learning.

In terms of the content, we kept that simple as well. The e-learning is the foundation piece, what we call the essentials. It covers what every marketer in Vodafone must know about the key topics, such as insights or brand or propositions, starting with the Vodafone definition of the particular marketing concept. It includes best practice case studies and examples, both from inside Vodafone and external; it covers our process, Vodafone's way of doing that particular thing; all backed up by key tools and templates that our marketers can start using immediately.

I'm really pleased by the results that we've seen thus far.

We've had over 25,000 visits to our academy in the 14 months that we've been live.

We have 12,000 regular users, over 10,000 online courses completed and over 700 marketers who have gone through the workshops as well. We use a Net Promoter Score to measure the success of the workshops and that's averaging over 90%, which is one of the highest scores we've ever seen at Vodafone. Given that it's an audience that demands high quality and there are very high expectations, we're very pleased by what we're seeing.

ANALYSED: THE VODAFONE ACADEMY

The situation

The need	There are four main reasons why marketing capability is so important for Vodafone: 1. Driving growth in a competitive market. 2. Generating efficiencies by adopting one, consistent way of marketing. 3. Becoming a hothouse for marketing talent. 4. Preparing for an even more competitive future.
The learning	The requirement is for ideas, processes and tools that can be applied consistently across Vodafone.
The learners	The audience has high expectations for the learning. They expect high-quality content that is practical and relevant to the day job.
The logistics	There are 4,000 marketers across more than 20 markets. Although the business language is English, for many marketers this is their second language.

The blend

	Methods	*Media*
Preparation	The programme is introduced to marketers through a one-hour briefing, led by their local Marketing Director.	Face to face backed up by email
Input	Self-paced, interactive materials allow marketers to orientate themselves around the key elements of the Vodafone way of marketing.	E-learning materials accessed through the portal
	A two-day workshop that allows marketers to experience the whole Vodafone way of marketing. This includes a competitive case study that teams present back to senior management. Each marketer and each team also develop action plans.	Face to face
Application	Senior managers review outputs from the two-day workshop and develop their own capability roadmap.	Face to face
	One month after the workshop, marketers are debriefed on the progress they have made with their action plans.	Teleconference
	Deep dive workshops on specific topics as required. These allow business teams to work together on real current problems.	Face to face
Follow-up	Marketers use the provided tools to systematise their use of the new Vodafone marketing processes.	Available online
	New case studies are published as they come available.	Online through the portal

PART 2
OVERVIEW

MORE THAN A JUKEBOX

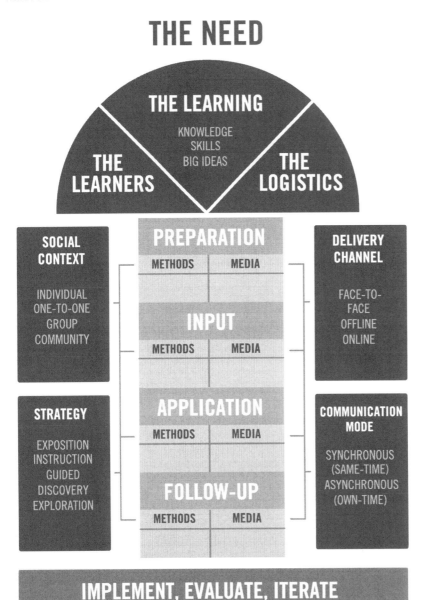

THE NEED

THE LEARNING
KNOWLEDGE
SKILLS
BIG IDEAS

THE LEARNERS

THE LOGISTICS

SOCIAL CONTEXT	PREPARATION		DELIVERY CHANNEL
INDIVIDUAL ONE-TO-ONE GROUP COMMUNITY	METHODS	MEDIA	FACE-TO-FACE OFFLINE ONLINE

	INPUT	
	METHODS	MEDIA

STRATEGY	APPLICATION		COMMUNICATION MODE
EXPOSITION INSTRUCTION GUIDED DISCOVERY EXPLORATION	METHODS	MEDIA	SYNCHRONOUS (SAME-TIME) ASYNCHRONOUS (OWN-TIME)

	FOLLOW-UP	
	METHODS	MEDIA

IMPLEMENT, EVALUATE, ITERATE

THIS IS THE JUKEBOX

You must admit – it does look a little like one.

The jukebox allows you to **disc**over the secrets of better blended learning in **record** time. That's if the terrible jokes don't put you off completely.

This chapter takes you through the *More Than* process from beginning to end, in a simplified form, without examples, anecdotes, arguments, case studies or any of the other material you will find elsewhere in this book.

As such, it acts as an overview and, later perhaps, as a refresher, but it is unlikely to win you over if you're starting from a sceptical position (and why shouldn't you be?). However, if you like plain talking, here it is.

1. THE NEED

Every design for a blended solution originates with a need that the designer believes some form of learning intervention can satisfy. Sometimes these needs stem from learners themselves, perhaps because they require the knowledge or skills to carry out a particular task, perhaps to gain a qualification or otherwise improve their employability, or perhaps for the simple love of learning.

Alternatively, the need could come from an employer looking to fix a problem, prepare for or adapt to a change, take advantage of an opportunity, or respond to a regulatory requirement. The momentum may also come from regional or national government, looking to address a skills gap and/or reduce unemployment.

At this very first stage, your initial concern is to make sure that training really is what's required to satisfy the need, and not some other performance intervention such as better information, more focused incentives or more up-to-date systems.

Once you are sure, the next priority is to home in on the performance requirement – what it is that learners need to be DOING differently if the need is to be satisfied.

By maintaining this emphasis on performance, you will avoid the trap of believing that the job is done simply because some training event has taken place.

2. THE THREE LS

The three Ls provide an easy-to-use framework for analysing the requirement for your intervention. Without thoroughly exploring each of these three dimensions, you can all too easily head off in the wrong direction. On the other hand, if you get your analysis right, your design can often fall easily into place.

The learning: First, focus in on the learning requirement. We've already asked what learners need to be doing differently if the underlying need is to be satisfied. We follow up by asking what they absolutely must know in order to do these things, what big ideas they need to understand and buy into, and what skills they need to acquire and/or put into practice.

The learners: If the learning represents our intended finishing point, the learners are where we start. You need to become familiar with your target audience: What expertise do they bring to the learning topic? How interested are they likely to be in learning about the topic? What hopes and fears will they bring to the learning experience? What cultural expectations will they have about the nature of any learning experience? What basic skills and computer literacy are they likely to have?

The logistics: Along your path from start to finish point, you will encounter barriers and opportunities, and you need to know exactly what these are: the numbers of learners; their locations and availability; the budget at your disposal; the deadlines; the people available to facilitate and support your solution; the equipment, tools and facilities.

3. PIAF

Like Edith Piaf, those using the Preparation-Input-Application-Follow-up structure for their solutions are likely to have 'no regrets'. Why? Because PIAF represents an end-to-end process, which only concludes when the original need has been satisfied.

Preparation: The purpose of the preparation phase is to align the learner with the intervention, so both are prepared to 'receive' each other.

Input: The input phase acts as a catalyst for action. It's usually the most formal part of the blend – the bit we commonly call a 'course', although it could be as simple as a coaching session.

Application: In the application phase, the learner applies what they have learned to real-life (or, where that's not possible, highly authentic tasks). In longer interventions, the input and application phases are likely to loop, so there are regular opportunities to apply what has been learned.

Follow-up: The follow-up phase is actually the longest, with the aim of embedding the learning into everyday behaviour. Throughout this phase, the learner is able to 'pull' from available resources, including coaches, experts, colleagues and content.

4. METHODS

At every phase in the intervention we need to select methods that will achieve the aims for that phase, given what we know about the three Ls – the learning, the learner and the logistics.

Learning methods are the tools we use to facilitate learning.

Importantly, they – and not technologies – are what determine whether a solution will be effective, which is why we have to get these right first.

A blended solution should not involve a trade-off between effectiveness and efficiency. The idea is to select an effective strategy and then – without compromise – choose the most streamlined mode of delivery. Quality is a given.

Learning methods are surprisingly timeless – Socrates would have had much the same choices available to him back in ancient Greece. Having said that, there are lots of available methods to choose from.

To make it easier to decide on the right methods, we can group them according to the **social context** in which they occur

(the learner alone, learning one-to-one, learning in a group and learning as part of a wider community) as well as the **strategies** that they employ (exposition, instruction, guided discovery and exploration). We'll be looking at those next.

5. BLENDING BY SOCIAL CONTEXT

Learning methods can be usefully categorised according to the social context in which they occur. Mixing social contexts within an intervention is one way in which you can blend.

Self-study is learning alone. It can range from reading a book, to practising playing a musical instrument, to engaging in a complex computer simulation.

One-to-one: We can learn one-to-one with an instructor, a coach, a mentor or a subject expert. This process can be conducted on-job, off-job or remotely.

Group: When we learn with a group, we expand the resources available to us as learners to include our fellow learners.

Community: Increasingly we reach out to a wider population to learn, beyond the small groups that we typically encounter in a formal learning setting. This form of learning could happen in a physical space (such as at a conference) but it is more likely to take place online.

Each of these social contexts has major advantages, but also some significant drawbacks. The art is to use each option in those situations in which its benefits are maximised and its limitations minimised.

6. BLENDING BY STRATEGY

Every learning solution, formal or informal, employs one or more of the following four basic strategies, whether or not anyone has consciously decided to use them:

Exposition is the simple delivery of information from subject expert to learner, typically as part of a formal syllabus. Examples include lectures, presentations and prescribed reading.

With **instruction**, a more systematic process is applied, starting with the formulation of specific learning objectives and culminating in some form of assessment. Instruction can take place in the classroom, through self-study e-learning or on the job.

Guided discovery is also a carefully structured process, but the emphasis here is on setting up activities from which the learner can gain their own insights and come to their own conclusions.

Exploration hands over control to the learner to make all the choices from available resources.

Different strategies will be suitable at different phases in an intervention and for different learning objectives and target populations. Mixing strategies is another form of blending.

7. MEDIA

At each phase of our blend, we will have chosen methods which we believe will lead to effective outcomes for our population of learners. Our next task is to decide how we will make each of those methods a reality, without compromising on their effectiveness. We deliver our methods using learning media.

Unlike methods, the range of media at our disposal is ever expanding, and the rate at which our options are increasing is accelerating. One hundred years ago, a teacher or trainer would have been restricted to face-to-face communication, a blackboard and printed materials. Their twenty-first century equivalents need to make sense of the potential provided by Twitter, smartphones, e-readers, YouTube, Skype and Wikipedia, to name just a few.

Each new medium that comes along offers us some fresh possibilities for greater efficiencies, improved flexibility and/or enhanced scalability.

But some are game changers – they make it possible to employ learning methods that previously would have been impractical to implement. For example, think of the reach provided by online social networks and the power of computer simulations.

To make it easier to select the most appropriate media, we can group them according to the **delivery channel** that they employ (face to face, offline – such as books or CDs – or online) as well as their **mode of communication** (occurring at a specific point in time or in the learner's own time). We'll be looking at these categories next.

8. BLENDING BY DELIVERY CHANNEL

Delivery channels provide the means for us to realise the methods that we have chosen. They enable the learner to access content and interact with teachers and fellow learners.

Face to face: Before the invention of the printing press, the only practical setting in which formal learning could take place was face to face. Even now, with many other options available, more teaching and training takes place face to face than by any other means, although this dominance is gradually diminishing.

Offline media: This term encompasses all those technologies that allow people to consume and interact with content in their own time but which do not require them to be connected to a network. Some common examples are books, CDs and DVDs.

Online media: Some online media are essentially forms of content, from simple web pages to elaborate 3D environments, simulations, e-learning modules and videos. Others provide the ability for Internet users to collaborate with each other, whether in their own time, as with social networks or forums, or in real-time, using tools such as Skype and web conferencing.

Through the delivery channels we use, we can make our intervention more scalable, flexible and efficient, however, this should never be at the expense of an effective solution. Mixing delivery channels is the third way in which you can blend.

9. BLENDING BY COMMUNICATION MODE

Each learning medium operates in one of two different modes. Synchronous (or 'same-time') communication requires that all parties be available at the same time. Asynchronous (or 'own-time') communication can be undertaken as and when it suits the participants.

Same-time: All learning originally took place face to face, and this form of communication is essentially synchronous – all participants need to be available at the same time. Technology has expanded our capacity for same-time communication, first through the telephone and now using tools like Skype on the Internet. As a means for learning, synchronous events provide a more immediate and responsive experience but at the expense of flexibility for individual learners.

Own-time: This mode of communication was originally dominated by the printed book, and later by various types of tapes and discs. The modern era has seen a dazzling array of new possibilities for self-paced consumption of content (think of the Wikipedia, YouTube and millions of other web sites) and asynchronous person-to-person interaction, including text messaging on mobile devices, email, discussion forums, wikis, blogs and social networks.

As the most flexible option, asynchronous communication is likely to constitute the primary mode for many blended solutions. However, synchronous events add immediacy and structure to an intervention, so a balance will often be desirable. Mixing communication modes is the fourth way in which you can blend.

10. IMPLEMENT, EVALUATE, ITERATE

Implement: A design is only a best guess at what will work in practice. Experience will obviously help but you can reduce the risk considerably by testing your ideas out with a representative sample of typical learners – not just at the end, when you're exhausted, the budget has run out and your deadline has passed, but at the start and at each key decision point that follows.

Evaluate: It is dangerous to think of a blended solution as a project that you can leave behind for another once it has been implemented. It will take some time to get a blend just right, so you will need to put the time in when it comes to evaluation. How effective has the solution been in meeting the need? How flexible and efficient is it proving in practice? How can it be refined to do an even better job?

Iterate: Blends are well suited to continuous improvement. Elements that are not working can be replaced by something different. New elements can be added and redundant material removed.

Think of a blend like a complex piece of hardware or a software application – something that is a perpetual work in progress. Each new version takes you one step closer to that perfect match between problem and solution.

THE

▶BL

COLLECTION:

WATERSTONES

THE WAT

ACADE

RSTONES

This case study provides an excellent example of blended learning in action within a highly competitive retail environment, providing development opportunities for staff while contributing to a strategic business change.

TALKING ABOUT THE WATERSTONES ACADEMY

Emma Brown, Head of Learning and Development, Waterstones

Waterstones is the largest book retailer in the UK. We started with one bookshop in Old Brompton Road 25 years ago. We now have 280 across the UK and Ireland.

A few years ago, Waterstones was sold by HMV group to a Russian billionaire, Alexander Mamut, and at that time we had a new Managing Director called James Daunt. He changed the direction and focus of the business, thinking about how individual shops could best suit the customers in local markets.

One of the main parts of the strategy that James wanted to drive was around a really strong offer with regards to digital and e-reading. So, we talked about creating a Waterstones Academy that would address the skills with which we needed to equip our booksellers. At the same time we were about to launch Kindles for our booksellers to sell.

Around this time I met with Rob Hubbard from LearningAge Solutions. Because I wanted to launch a Waterstones Academy, we had discussed what we wanted that to look like. I was very clear about the things I really didn't want on a website, having worked with e-learning in the past.

**Rob Hubbard, Founder,
LearningAge Solutions**

Working with Emma was fantastic in that she was very good at saying what she wanted to achieve but then trusted us as the digital learning experts to come up with the best way of doing that.

We worked really closely with Emma and her team and with booksellers themselves throughout the whole design and development process. We needed to make sure that what we were sketching out initially, what we were prototyping, what we were mocking up and then what we were building was absolutely right for the organisation, but most importantly for the users.

Emma

So we talked about what the Waterstones Academy needed to do. With the announcement that we were about to start selling Amazon Kindle devices, the need for the Academy accelerated. We wanted to launch with digital training, but we also knew that we wanted the Academy to have much greater functionality beyond that, because we wanted to also roll out an accredited Certificate in Bookselling in the future.

The good thing about the fact that we were launching Kindle meant that every shop was going to get wi-fi and we managed to negotiate that every shop would also get a Kindle Fire HD through which to access the Academy. It opened up the possibilities of what we could actually do with the Academy – we could show videos and use sound, whereas previously we wouldn't have been able to do that when we were using the shops' PCs.

Rob

At its heart, Waterstone's Academy is a goal-based learning system, so instead of going through a one-size-fits-all course, people work towards goals that are going to help them improve their performance. It's a much more targeted, tailored and practical way of learning, particularly for skills.

Emma

A bookseller's experience of the Academy would start pretty much when they join Waterstones. They can register on the site themselves. They can access it on their smart phones, from home or at work on their Kindle Fire – essentially wherever they want to.

When they access the site, they see a variety of 'shields' that are relevant to their role. So, as a new bookseller, for example, they would see the induction shield. They would work through that, looking at various goals and related activities that would give them an introduction to life at Waterstones and their role.

At its heart, Waterstone's Academy is a goal-based learning system

Later on, they might use the site to take part in our Certificate in Bookselling programme, a qualification that's accredited by the University of Derby.

Booksellers can do their performance review on the Academy site as well, because I really wanted it to become a one-stop shop for development, engagement and performance.

Overall, the results that we've had have been incredibly encouraging and the Academy has been a really, really invaluable tool for the business.

We've also had fantastic feedback from booksellers who have gone through the Certificate in Bookselling, as well as from managers about how well people are applying what they are learning and how this is reflected in our sales results.

Typical learner feedback
'I now feel even more responsible for ensuring the success of the store and achieving everything I can whilst being fully equipped with some of the fundamentals of being a good bookseller.'

'You should be really proud of the work you and your team have just put into the Academy. I've just completed the digital shield and it's one of the best training tools I've ever used. I think it's going to prove really valuable during this next phase of business.'

Overall, the results that we've had have been incredibly encouraging and the Academy has been a really, really invaluable tool for the business.

ANALYSED: THE CERTIFICATE IN BOOKSELLING

The situation

The need	Waterstones, like all specialist book retailers, needs to respond to the shift to online sales and digital reading. They need to upgrade the skills of retail employees to provide a service to customers that cannot be matched elsewhere.
The learning	Booksellers need to know the key titles and authors in a wide range of genres to suit different customer types. They also need knowledge of the wider industry.
	The Certificate also needed to convey a number of big ideas about bookselling, e.g. that service is at the heart of the customer experience; the need for energy, pace and a positive attitude.
	The skills element varied from the practical, e.g. visual merchandising, to the interpersonal, e.g. interpreting and responding to customer behaviour.
The learners	The Certificate is open to 3,000 employees, of which 250 had graduated at the time of writing.
	Booksellers are highly educated and the Certificate needed to appeal to them at an intellectual level.
The logistics	It was not possible to take booksellers off the shop floor, so they had to use some of their own time for studying and, where possible, the activities needed to be work-based.
	A tight budget meant that most of the work to design and deliver the Certificate had to be carried out in-house.

The blend

	Methods	*Media*
Preparation	Marketing for each new year's enrolment is carried out through Internal Comms.	Waterstones intranet and other channels
	Each applicant is assigned the induction module. This explains what will be expected of them if they undertake the Certificate programme.	Waterstones Academy website
	Applicants speak with their line managers to obtain sign-off.	Face to face
	Applicants submit a proposal explaining why they should be on the programme.	Through the Academy website
Input	There are three modules, each of which lasts three months. Each module contains: • reading • links to articles and books • case study videos / acted demonstrations, etc.	All accessed through the Academy website, which is accessible on all devices
Application	Each module includes some individual critiques and reflections, on which the tutor provides feedback.	Through the Academy website
	Learners are assigned to cohorts of 10 as a basis for group activities. For example, each learner creates a commercial display and submits a photo of this for review by others in the cohort.	The activities take place on the job, but are then submitted and reviewed through the Academy site

	Methods	*Media*
Follow-up	When all three modules are completed, the learner submits a final reflection on their learning and makes plans for future application – essentially a new 'contract', which is tied in with the performance review.	Through the Academy website
	The Certificate is awarded on the basis of competency not an exam.	
	The learner can then move on to the Senior Bookseller and Lead Bookseller Certificates. The combination of the three earns the learner a degree.	

PART 3
ANALYSIS

WE START BY ANALYSING THE SITUATION

In this and following parts of this book we explore in more detail the key stages in the systematic approach to the design of blended solutions; solutions that have the potential to prove not only effective in meeting the need, but also efficient, flexible and scalable. These stages can be summarised as follows:

- analysing the unique characteristics of the situation for which the solution is being designed;

- determining what needs to be done in terms of Preparation, Input, Application and Follow-up (PIAF) to meet the demands of this situation;

- selecting the most appropriate methods for each of the four phases of PIAF, taking account of what we believe will be the most effective learning strategies and social contexts;

- determining the learning media best suited to delivering each of these methods, taking account of what we believe will be the most appropriate delivery channels and communication modes.

This might sound abstract and theoretical, but stick with it, because the process can be quickly and easily applied in practice.

We start with the first step in the process – analysing the situation. This step comes first because the information we uncover at this stage underpins just about every decision we make when it comes to design. In fact, determining the solution can sometimes seem pretty obvious once you have the right information at your disposal.

There are four aspects of the situation that we need to understand:

The need: Every design for a blended solution starts with one or more underlying needs, whether these originate from organisations or learners. Your task is to understand the need as well as you can and then determine whether a learning intervention is going to make a positive contribution to meeting the need.

The learning: By this we mean the end point that we're aiming towards with our solution. Remember that, while we may regard learning as our aim, the project sponsor is likely to be much more concerned with what this learning might achieve in terms of increased performance. If we can focus in on performance, then this will serve us well when we come to making design decisions.

The learners: Under this heading we include all the information that we need to know about the population at which our intervention will be targeted. You could say that if 'the learning' represents the end result that we are looking to achieve, 'the learners' are where we start. Our design essentially bridges the gap between the skills, knowledge and other attributes that learners have now and what they will need to have if they are to support the strategic goal of the organisation.

The logistics: Of course, no design is ever created without constraints. Under this heading we take account of time, budget, geography and all sorts of other factors that will help or hinder us in bridging the learning gap.

In the following chapters we will explore these four aspects of the situation in more detail.

CLARIFYING THE NEED

START WITH THE GOAL

Before we get too excited about the prospect of designing a new learning solution, it is vitally important that we clarify what need, goal or impediment is driving the requirement. Depending on the context in which you work, the need may originate with learners themselves, with an employer or with government.

- **Learners** may be driving the intervention, perhaps because they are looking to acquire the knowledge and skills needed to perform a task, perhaps to gain a qualification or otherwise improve their employability, or perhaps because they simply love learning. If you run public courses for a college or an independent training provider, then learners are your customers and you will be keen to respond to their requirements.

- **An employer** may be driving the intervention, looking to fix a problem, prepare employees for a change, take advantage of an opportunity, or respond to a regulatory requirement. If you work as a learning professional inside an organisation then the needs of your organisation are likely to be paramount.

- **A regional or national government** or some similar organisation may also be driving the intervention, perhaps to address a current or potential skills gap and/or to reduce unemployment. Governments may intervene in vocational training by providing funding to colleges, independent training providers, employers or learners themselves.

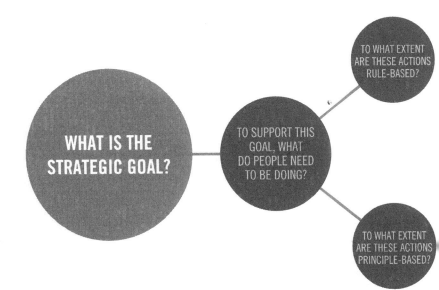

FOCUS ON PERFORMANCE

Once you have established the goal for the programme, a good second question to ask is *what it is that people need to be doing in the future that they may not be doing now if this goal is to be achieved.* You are looking for specific, observable behaviours, for example:

- Use the in-house social networking tool to seek out expertise and resolve challenges.

- Recognise and act upon opportunities for upselling.

- Avoid waste by re-using …

- Drive with consideration for other road users.

- Develop PowerPoint slides that act as genuine visual aids rather than speaker prompts.

- Use the principles of :.. to drive decision-making and actions in their work.

By maintaining an emphasis on performance rather than learning, you will avoid the trap of believing that the job is done simply because some training event has taken place.

What matters is not so much what people learn, but what they do with that learning.

WHAT SORT OF PERFORMANCE?

It can be helpful, even at this early stage, to consider the nature of the actions that you want people to be taking. To what extent is the performance *rule-based* or *principle-based?*

Rule-based tasks are algorithmic and repetitive. As long as you follow the rules, you'll get the job done to a consistent quality. These are tasks like replacing a punctured tyre, completing a form or operating a cash register. You can teach these tasks using simple instruction – see a demonstration, have a go, get feedback, and so on.

The trouble is that fewer and fewer of the tasks that we have to perform at work are rule-based. After all, if tasks are algorithmic, the temptation is to find a robot or a computer to do them, or to look for the cheapest possible source of labour, wherever that is in the world. Much of the work we now do in organisations is *heuristic* – it requires us to make judgements based on principles. Principles are not black and white – they need to be experienced rather than taught. And as we shall see later, with principle-based tasks, we're much better off using a strategy of guided discovery.

It will be unlikely that the performance you are looking to elicit is entirely rule-based or entirely principle-based – most jobs involve a mixture of the two. However, it will help you to know roughly where the balance lies as you start to investigate options for your solution.

What matters is not so much
what people learn, but what
they do with that learning.

IS LEARNING THE ANSWER?

We cannot always take a requirement for a learning solution at face value – our project sponsor may be wrongly diagnosing the problem. Work performance is influenced by many factors, as this diagram shows[8]:

First of all, performers are influenced by the situation in which they are working: do they have clear objectives, authority and responsibilities; the necessary time, budget, information, tools and other resources; appropriate working conditions?

When we look at the performers themselves, do they have the necessary aptitudes for the task? No amount of training is going to make a square peg fit in a round hole. It is possible that the recruitment and selection process has broken down and people need to be allocated to more suitable work.

Motivation is another important determinant of performance. To an extent, a learning intervention can impact on motivation, not least because we are all driven by the desire to master

our chosen job, but this is not the primary goal of learning. Inappropriate incentives and disincentives may be impacting on motivation and we will not be able to influence these through our intervention.

Finally, performance cannot flourish if the performer is not receiving timely, relevant and specific feedback on their performance, whether this is targeted or incidental.

If we are confident that learning is at least *part* of what is required if we are to achieve the underlying goal, we can move on to analysing the situation in more detail. If learning is really not a causal factor, we can politely take our leave and let other specialists address the problem.

On to the three Ls ...

8_ This model was influenced by a Kepner-Tregoe workshop I attended some 35 years ago. I hope I've remembered it correctly.

THE FIRST L:
THE LEARNING

In the previous chapter we saw that our initial priority when considering a new learning intervention was to establish the nature of the underlying need. We focused on performance by asking what our target population would have to be doing differently if the need was to be satisfied. We checked whether factors other than knowledge, skills and attitudes were getting in the way of this performance, so we did not waste resources on a learning intervention when learning was not really any part of the problem.

Let's suppose that you have got past this stage and still feel comfortable that you, as a learning professional, are the right person to be addressing the problem. Your next task is to come to terms with **the three Ls** – the learning (the immediate outcome of your intervention), the learners (your starting point) and the logistics (what will help and hinder you along the way).

In this chapter we address the first of the Ls, the learning.

THREE TYPES OF LEARNING

There are many ways of categorising learning. It does not matter too much which model you choose, as long as you can see a clear relationship between the type of learning you are attempting to achieve and the strategies that you select to get you there. For the purposes of blended learning design, we've chosen a variant on the familiar KSA model (knowledge, skills and attitudes), because we've tried it time and time again and it gets us where we want to go.

So, you've already established what it is that your learners need to be *doing* that they may not be doing now. To understand the learning requirement, we need to follow this up by asking:

- what they absolutely *must* know in order to do these things

- what big ideas they need to understand and buy into, and

- what skills they need to acquire and/ or put into practice

If we dig deep enough then the answers to these three questions will tell us everything we need to know about the learning.

We'll start with knowledge and its close relative, information.

KNOWLEDGE AND INFORMATION

Knowledge and information are not quite the same thing. Knowledge is information that has been committed to memory, so it can be recalled without the need to refer to some external resource. This is an important distinction when you're analysing requirements. It's essential you find out what really needs to be remembered and what can be safely looked up as and when needed. There is a definite change in people's expectations in this respect, because it has become so easy to search for information online on a PC or a mobile device that it seems pointless to try and remember everything that's relevant to your job. In designing your solution, you'll want to pick out

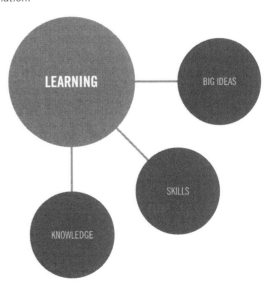

those items of information that someone really *must* know if they are to perform effectively in their job. The rest – the *nice to know* and the *where to go* – you can provide as a resource.

Perhaps the greatest danger when analysing requirements is to over-estimate the amount of knowledge that people are going to need. The main culprits are subject specialists who have long since forgotten what it's like to be novices in their particular fields and think just about everything that they know will be interesting to learners and important for them to know.

A good way to resist this pressure is to ask the question: 'What's the absolute minimum that learners need to know before they can start practising this task?'

Again, this keeps the focus on performance. Generally speaking, employers are much less interested in what you know that in what you can do.

Of course there are some occupations in which it is absolutely essential that the job holders have a great deal of knowledge, so they can respond immediately to difficult and sometimes dangerous situations. The examples that are usually quoted are airline pilots and surgeons. Yes, they need to have an excellent understanding of the concepts and principles that underpin their decision-making within their narrow specialism. Yes, they need to know exactly

what the correct procedures should be in everyday situations. But, they can – and do – refer to reference documentation in extraordinary situations. In other occupations the ratio of 'must know' to 'must know where to look or who to ask' will be heavily weighted to the latter.

Be careful to distinguish *explicit knowledge*, which can be easily articulated and assessed, from *tacit knowledge*, which is much harder to teach formally. Tacit knowledge explains how things work – what causes things to happen and what is likely to happen if we decide to do this as opposed to that. Another way of thinking of tacit knowledge is as *wisdom* and, as the term implies, this tends to be hard earned over time.

A good way to resist this pressure is to ask the question: 'What's the absolute minimum that learners need to know before they can start practising this task?'

If this is what you find out ...	... then this is the implication
There is a 'must know' requirement	In most cases, an instruction strategy will work best. Reinforce regularly and don't expect too much too quickly.
There is information which it would be nice for people to know	Use an exploration strategy. Suggest resources that people are likely to find useful.
Some information must be available for quick reference	Your solution must include an easy access reference component. For those people who do not work at a desk, consider using mobile devices.
There is a need for tacit knowledge	Make sure your solution incorporates an experiential element (learning from doing the job) and a social element (learning from others who are doing the job). Don't expect this to happen in a hurry.

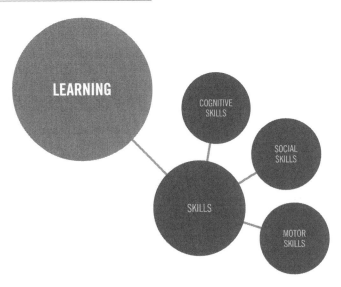

SKILLS

Skills matter a great deal more at work than knowledge. Skills are your abilities to do things, to put procedural knowledge into practice. As such, they directly impact on performance. There is really only one way to acquire skills and that is through practice, ideally with the aid of specific, timely, relevant and reliable feedback.

If there is one consistent fault with the training programmes that most organisations provide, it is an over-emphasis on theoretical knowledge and a wholly inadequate provision for practice with feedback.

By far the most successful training technique is to provide just the most essential information up-front and then to get the learner practising. You can feed in more 'nice to know' information as the learner begins to build confidence.

If there is one consistent fault with the training programmes that most organisations provide, it is an over-emphasis on theoretical knowledge and a wholly inadequate provision for practice with feedback.

The ultimate aim of skills development is for the learner to be able to apply the skill correctly without any conscious effort. Whether it's playing the piano, programming in JavaScript, closing a sale or hitting a top-spin backhand, the goal of unconscious competence is obtainable by almost anybody who puts in enough effort. Research suggests that world-class performance of skills as varied as sports, playing an instrument and mathematics is obtainable by anyone who has the mental or physical aptitude for those skills (you'll not be good at basketball if you are five foot six and you will not excel at maths with a low intelligence) if you put in 10,000 hours of practice. While few of us can afford to devote that much time to developing a skill, our aspirations probably do not extend to being a world-class performer and not all skills are that difficult to perfect. In practice, we need 'good enough' more often than we need world class.

From the point of view of designing blended solutions, what really makes the most difference is to determine the type of skill that needs developing. In particular, you need to know with whom or with what the learner will be interacting when they apply this skill:

Motor skills: In this case the learner is *interacting with the physical world*, for example: lifting a heavy object, driving a car, using a mouse. While these tasks can sometimes be simulated, as with flying a plane, more often than not we have to provide opportunities for practice with the real object in a realistic situation.

Interpersonal skills: Here the learner is *interacting with people*, as they would if they were making a sale, providing someone with feedback or making a presentation. Interpersonal tasks can be simulated – and this may be useful as an early form of practice – but no computer can yet accurately provide feedback on what a learner says or on their body language. So, to be really confident about a learner's interpersonal skills, you'll have to provide opportunities for practice with other people.

Cognitive skills: In this case the learner is *interacting with information*. Lots of our tasks at work are like this, requiring us to solve problems and make decisions. Examples include business planning, using software, solving quadratic equations, writing reports, or reviewing financial data. Cognitive skills lend themselves more easily to computer-based practice.

Of course, you're quite likely to find there's a need for a mix of different skills – motor, interpersonal and cognitive. This is another powerful reason why blended learning can be so useful – there simply isn't one method or medium that meets the whole need.

If this is what you find out ...	... then this is the implication
There is a need for motor skills	You may be lucky enough to have access to a simulator to provide early practice. Otherwise, you'll need to set up practice in an authentic physical environment, with the opportunity for the learner to obtain feedback.
There is a need for interpersonal skills	You might be able to provide initial practice with interactive computer-based scenarios, but the learner will have to graduate to practising with other people, with the opportunity to obtain feedback.
There is a need for cognitive skills	You may be able to find or develop software that will allow the learner to obtain repeated practice of the skill. Otherwise, you will need to contrive other forms of activity that allow the learner to get feedback from another person.
There is a need for a broad range of skills	While it is important that you clearly separate out the types of skills and allow the learner to practise them individually, real job performance is likely to involve all the skills being applied together. That means you must also provide regular opportunities for the learner to practise the whole task.

BIG IDEAS

We mentioned earlier that some tasks are rule-based – they can be carried out routinely in accordance with established procedures. Other tasks require us to make critical judgements in highly variable situations, and the basis on which we do this – in the absence of rules – is to rely on our understanding of cause and effect: if we do this, *x* is likely to occur, whereas if we do that, *y* will occur.

A principle is a statement of cause and effect. It sums up what we believe is likely to be the cause of a particular phenomenon or the outcome of a particular action. Principles govern our problem-solving and decision-making, whether consciously or unconsciously.

Generally speaking, it is not enough to *know* a principle ('smoking is bad for you', 'a meeting will be more effective with a clear objective', 'organisations benefit from diversity', 'object-oriented code is easier to maintain') for us to act on it; we really need to *buy in* to the idea. And we are much more likely to buy in to an idea that we feel we have discovered for ourselves. That's why principles are much better acquired through a process of guided discovery than through simple instruction.

We cannot leave an analysis of learning requirements without mentioning attitudes. An attitude is a predisposition, a tendency to think, feel or act in a certain way without reference to the facts of the situation. Attitudes can get in the way of people buying in to key principles and so have to be addressed by your solution. Your whole programme will be a wasted effort if you cannot get past attitudes such as "I absolutely hate computers", "My job would be perfect if only there were no customers", "I would never give a task like that to a woman" or "E-learning is the work of the devil."

If this is what you find out ...	... then this is the implication
There is a need for learners to understand and buy in to one or more big ideas	Be quite clear what these ideas are. Try to think of activities that will allow learners to figure out the sense of the idea for themselves.
There is a need to tackle negative attitudes	Tackle these early on and you'll remove the barriers to your big ideas. Have learners articulate their negative attitudes without judging them. Provide activities that might trigger cognitive dissonance[9] ('I take drugs, I'm a fan of David Beckham, David Beckham doesn't take drugs – this conflict is uncomfortable').

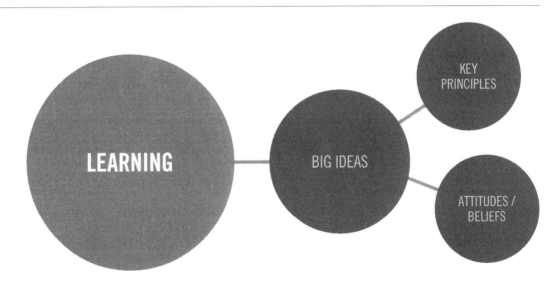

9_ In psychology, cognitive dissonance is the mental stress or discomfort experienced by an individual who holds two or more contradictory beliefs, ideas, or values at the same time, or is confronted by new information that conflicts with existing beliefs, ideas, or values.

THE SECOND L:
THE LEARNERS

If the first L – the learning – represents our intended finishing point, the second L – the learners – is where we start. It is essential that you get to know your target audience. What expertise will they bring to the learning topic? How interested are they likely to be in learning about the topic? What hopes and fears will they have about the learning experience? What cultural expectations will they have about the nature of a learning experience? What basic skills and computer literacy are they likely to have?

EVERY LEARNER IS DIFFERENT

There's a lot of talk in learning and development circles about learning styles, the purpose of which is to help teachers, trainers and designers of learning experiences to adapt their work to reflect the characteristics of different types of learners. This seems a reasonable endeavour until you reflect on the fact that there are literally hundreds of competitive models, which cannot, of course, all be right, and that not one of these has so far come through any critical test of its validity.

The Association of Psychological Science concluded that:

'There is no adequate evidence base to justify incorporating learning-styles assessments into general educational practice.'

And in the UK, a review by The Learning and Skills Research Centre found the various theories 'seriously wanting' and with 'serious deficiencies'. Many were downright dangerous as they 'over-simplify, label and stereotype'. Both Donald Clark[9] and Will Thalheimer[10] have reviewed this research in some detail in their blogs – don't bother checking these out if you're a learning styles enthusiast unless you have a thick skin.

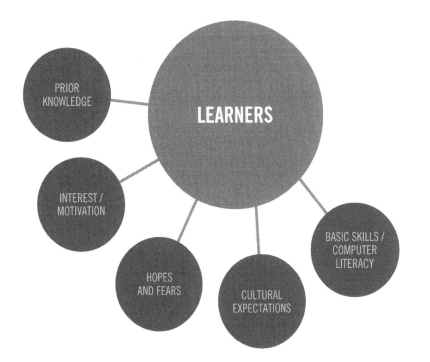

9_ http://donaldclarkplanb.blogspot.co.uk/

10_ You can earn $5K if you can apply learning styles in a learning intervention and prove that it improves the result. No one has in the 8 years it's been running. See http://www.willatworklearning.com/2014/08/learning-styles-challenge-year-eight.html

The fact that we have yet to find a reliable way to categorise learners, does not reduce the need for a learner-centred approach to design or for empathetic teaching. As Dr John Medina makes clear in *Brain Rules*, every one of the world's seven billion inhabitants is different:

'What you do in life physically changes what your brain looks like.'

'Our brains are so sensitive to external inputs that their physical wiring depends upon the culture in which they find themselves.'

'Learning results in physical changes to the brain and these changes are unique to each individual.'

Interesting as all this is, it does not take us that far in terms of the big decisions we have to make when designing a blended solution. There are two learner characteristics that are far more influential than learning preferences. One is the extent of their prior learning, and the other is their motivation to learn about the subject in question.

If this is what you find out …	… then this is the implication
You have an audience with widely differing preferences	Provide alternative options if you can within your budget, but never at the expense of what is needed to meet your learning objectives.
You have an audience with broadly similar preferences	Be happy.

THE IMPORTANCE OF PRIOR LEARNING

As we've discussed above, learning, both formal and informal, literally rewires the brain. The more a person learns about something – a work task or a subject of interest – the more elaborate become the mental models (known by academics as schemas) that connect the various underlying concepts and principles. These models provide us with an understanding of how all the elements of a domain fit together and, as a result, enable us to solve problems and make decisions. After a while, we become so competent in a particular aspect of our lives that we seem to respond to situations intuitively – in other words without conscious effort.

When we know very little about a subject, we have very little prior knowledge to connect to. Without pre-existing schemas to build on, we need examples, stories, metaphors and similes to help us relate new information to our other life experiences. Most novices will crave a well-structured and supported programme of learning, which allows them plenty of time to process new information and to make sense of this in the context of practical application. They need reassurance and encouragement to help them through the difficulties they will inevitably encounter. In short, novices appreciate and benefit from good teaching and should, as a result, be the main focus of your attention.

All learning is a process of establishing patterns and making connections.

The more expert you already are in a particular area, the less structure and support you need to learn something new related to that area. We all have aspects of our life that we understand really well, whether or not we could easily explain what it is that we know to someone else. We may be an expert in molecular biology, photography, accounting, office politics, bringing up children or the tactics of football. Because of our understanding, we can pretty well cope with any new information relating to our specialisms. We are very hard to overwhelm or overload, because we can easily relate new information to what we already know; we can sort out the credible from the spurious and the important from the trivial. As an expert, we can cope with a long lecture, a densely written textbook, a forum with thousands of postings, or a whole heap of links returned in response to a search query.

These are the extremes. Of course there are many gradations of expertise and only a minority of learners are complete novices or acknowledged experts. But it is easy to see how, if we are not careful, we end up providing an 'average' learning experience which satisfies no-one.

We can over-teach those who already have a lot of expertise:

* We patronise them with over-simplified metaphors, examples and case studies.

* We frustrate them by holding back important information, which we then proceed to reveal on a careful step-by-step basis.

* We insult them by forcing them to undergo unnecessary assessments.

* We waste their time by forcing them to participate in collaborative activities with those who know much less than they do.

And we can under-teach the novices:

* We bombard them with information that they cannot hope to process, providing nowhere near enough time for consolidation.

* We provide insufficient examples and case studies to help them relate new information to their past experience.

* We are not always there when they get stuck or have questions.

* We do not go far enough in providing practical activities that will help them to turn interesting ideas into usable skills.

It may seem from this that you need to double your workload by providing two versions of each learning experience, but it doesn't work like that. The relative experts need resources not courses and, of the two, resources are much easier to assemble. Many times you can just point the expert at the information and let them get on with it. And by doing this, you've reduced the population that requires a more formal learning experience considerably. You can start to give the novices the attention they deserve.

If this is what you find out ...	... then this is the implication
You have an audience of relative novices.	Be careful not to overload them. Provide them with plenty of support. In terms of strategies, focus on instruction and guided discovery at the expense of exposition and exploration.
You have an audience with relatively good prior knowledge.	Minimise structure and hand-holding. Back off and allow them to control what they learn and how.
You have a mixed audience in terms of prior knowledge.	Concentrate on the novices. Direct those with more prior knowledge towards the resources.

THE MOTIVATION TO LEARN

Another characteristic that will have a big influence on your design is the degree of motivation the target population is likely to have to learn about the topic in question. It is hard to bring about learning without a degree of emotional engagement.

Quite simply, when our attention is aroused we remember much more.

If you know that learners will be coming to your programme full of enthusiasm, you have the luxury of being able to get straight on with the teaching, without much in the way of preliminaries. More often, learners need some convincing that they should devote time in their busy lives to what you have to teach. It is possible they have no choice about whether or not they go through your programme and are feeling just a bit resentful. In situations like this you have to build into your design the steps necessary to overcome these obstacles. You need to show why the topic in question is relevant to the learner's life and why time spent engaging with it will yield real benefits.

Attention also needs to be given to the learner's hopes and fears, factors that can be easily overlooked when you are focusing entirely on performance. Very often the learner's primary motivation is to fit in and to avoid embarrassment, particularly when they are new in a job and lacking in confidence. It is very important that these hopes and fears are taken into account when designing your solution.

If this is what you find out ...	*... then this is the implication*
Your population will come to you motivated to learn	One less thing to worry about.
Your population may be indifferent to what you have to offer or, worse, reluctant to engage	Do everything you can to help learners see the benefit of your programme. Ideally they will feel that they have discovered this for themselves rather than being sold.
Some of your population are motivated and some are not	If you can, address the two elements of your population separately. More likely, you will need to progress on the basis that nobody is motivated.

OF COURSE IT'S NOT THAT SIMPLE

We have concentrated on two characteristics that seem to have the biggest impact on your design – prior learning and the motivation to learn – but learners are more complex than that. You'll want to find out as much information about your target population as you can, for example:

- There will be cultural differences, from country to country and organisation to organisation, particularly in terms of the expectations that learners are likely to have about the way that formal learning is carried out. You may have to adapt your solution to take account of differences between, say, South Americans and the Chinese, but be wary of stereotypes.

- Learners will have different expectations about the nature of formal learning based on their past experience, perhaps at school or college, perhaps in their previous employment. Sudden, unexplained changes will, naturally enough, be met with bewilderment, maybe hostility.

- Be aware of any potential problems in terms of computer literacy, particularly if your solution is likely to make use of technology. In extreme cases, it may be necessary for the computer illiterate to have special training to overcome this obstacle, before they participate in your solution.

- Be aware of practical obstacles, such as childcare responsibilities, which may hinder learners from travelling to training events.

- Take account of the extent and nature of any disabilities among your target population. In many cases you will find that you are bound by law to make your solution accessible to everyone, but there are moral and practical considerations as well, not least the fact that a relatively large proportion of the population who want to engage in learning and development is affected by some form of disability.

PUTTING THIS INFORMATION TO USE

If this is what you find out …	*… then this is the implication*
Your population is culturally disposed to low levels of interaction in a classroom context	Adapt your classroom events accordingly, without sacrificing your chances of reaching your objectives. You could avoid the classroom altogether and provide alternative means for interaction elsewhere in your blend.
Your population is used to traditional means for learning.	If you intend to make changes, try to integrate some familiar, traditional methods alongside the new. Make sure to consult with the population beforehand and explain how the changes will benefit them.
Some or all of your population have low levels of computer literacy.	Deal with this first as a separate learning intervention.
Some of your population have a difficulty in attending classroom events away from their normal place of work.	Take this into account when determining the media you will use. Try to be flexible.
Some of your population have a visual, hearing or other impairment.	Where possible, make your solution accessible to all. Where this is not practical, provide an alternative approach especially for those who are unable to access some aspect of your solution.

THE THIRD L:
THE LOGISTICS

ALL DESIGN TAKES PLACE WITHIN CONSTRAINTS

The third element of the situation that you need to investigate, after the learning requirements ('the learning') and the characteristics of the target population ('the learner'), is the logistics. You need to know what practical constraints (or to put it more positively, what opportunities) you will have to accommodate (or, in the case of opportunities, exploit).

BUDGET

TIME

FACILITATORS

AUDIENCE NUMBERS / LOCATIONS / AVAILABILITY

EQUIPMENT / FACILITIES / TOOLS

LOGISTICS

All design takes place within constraints.

Quite possibly, the film director James Cameron moans about his measly $200m budget and his unreasonable two-year schedule.

Chances are you have much greater limitations to work with, but this is completely normal, and can be seen to help the design process by closing down the options you need to consider.

Quite possibly, the film director James Cameron moans about his measly $200m budget and his unreasonable two-year schedule.

So what logistical factors are likely to impact on your design?

- The size and geographic distribution of the target population.

- The amount of time available for training.

- The budget.

- The deadline.

- The facilities and equipment available.

- The human resources available for design, development and delivery, and the skills and knowledge they possess.

- The availability of subject specialists.

- The software tools available for development and delivery.

- The organisation's policies and procedures with regard to learning and development.

- What incentives there are for performing.

It is important to remember that, whatever constraints you may have, your primary goal is effectiveness and that any compromises you make must be made in light of the commitment to quality.

If this is what you find out ...	... then this is the implication
You have a relatively small target population	Unless the potential value of the improved or changed performance is high, you may not be able to justify developing special materials. Look to use what is already available.
You have a relatively large target population	You can afford to invest in high-quality self-study materials that can be delivered cheaply. Look for approaches that do not depend on the continual involvement of teachers, trainers and facilitators.
You have a relatively small budget	Double your efforts to look for the most efficient and scalable means for development and delivery. Make the best possible use of available technologies and existing materials. You could also consider reducing the scope of what you are aiming to achieve.
You have a relatively large budget	Amaze people. You could consider coming in under budget rather than waste resources. You might also invest more in resources that will provide long-term support to learners.
You are working to a tight deadline	Be prepared to cut down the scope of what you are aiming to achieve. Concentrate on the high-priority requirements and deal with these thoroughly rather than spread your resources too thinly.
Your deadline is relatively relaxed	Use the time, not to slow down your efforts but to consult more widely and to test out your ideas and your prototypes with your target population.
You do not have access to the facilities and/or equipment that you need	If you cannot hire in what you need, look for alternative delivery methods that do not place the same demands on facilities and equipment.
You are short of human resources to design, develop and deliver your solution	Not much you can do here except make efficient use of the resources you do have and hire in the expertise you need, budget permitting.

If this is what you find out ...	... then this is the implication
You are restricted in the access you have to subject specialists	Try to make efficient use of the time you have with subject experts and plan their time well in advance. Hopefully they will not insist on approving the design at every stage.
You do not have the software you would like for the development and delivery of your solution	Make a case for buying the software, particularly if it will add capability or improve efficiency. Otherwise consider renting or subscribing to it on a temporary basis.
Your organisation's learning and development policies restrict you from doing what you want	Put forward a case for change, based on evidence of success in other organisations. Offer to do a small-scale pilot to prove that your approach will work.

AN ANALYSIS IS NOT FOR EVER

With this information to hand, you are now in a good position to make design decisions, but be prepared to revisit your analysis because situations are always changing and new information comes available all the time. Design is – and should be – an iterative process as you strive to ever more closely meet the needs of your project sponsors and your ultimate customers – the learners.

THE

BL

COLLECTION:

CARNIVAL UK

ALL ABOARD

AT CARNIVAL UK

With this solution you'll see how the blended approach can be adapted to the trickiest of training environments. In particular, note how the design allows learners to obtain key knowledge at their own pace, freeing up trainers to provide coaching and personalised instruction in the workplace – in this case on board a cruise liner in the middle of the ocean.

TALKING ABOUT INDUCTION TRAINING FOR CREWMEMBERS

John Allen, Head of Deck & Technical Training at Carnival UK

Carnival UK is the provider of Cunard and P&O cruises. As part of the Carnival Corporation we are the largest vacation company in the world.

The main reason for us to change our induction programme was to improve its effectiveness. We take crew members from all over the world, they fly to this country, we ship them to Southampton and put them on board a ship. It could be their first time and we have to train them in all the safety activities that go along with shipboard duties. For someone who's really tired or jetlagged to then sit through an entire training programme wasn't proving to be that effective. We wanted to change the whole approach and give people much more of a heads-up before they got on board of what ship life is going to be like, and also what the safety duties involve.

The learners are spread right across the spectrum. We have people that come from all over the world, particularly India and the Philippines. English is not necessarily their first language. We're dealing with everybody that needs to be on board the ship, whether that's the master of the ship or the people that work back of house in the laundry or the galley. We have up to 2,000 people to train on each of the larger vessels.

One of the constraints we have working on a ship is that we don't have Internet connectivity all the time. While the ship is in satellite range we can have some connectivity but the priority is for our passengers to access wi-fi as that's part of their holiday experience. Another constraint is that we don't have much time with crewmembers. We're mandated by legislation as to how long they can work on board a ship and time spent training is considered to be working time. The primary need is to to be safe, serve the passengers and give that great holiday experience but somewhere in between we've got to give the training that provides the extra benefits that we offer with the brand.

Phillip Bowler - Fleet Safety Training Manager at Carnival UK

How the new training starts off is people are assigned a pre-employment package. Within a certain amount of days they have to complete an online assessment, which comes with a full package of computer-based training (CBT). They're doing that at their own pace, in their own time, in their own house or wherever they happen to get the Internet connection. Nowadays, everybody's familiar with the technology. We haven't experienced any problems yet with the CBT. It's set up so it's very simple for them to navigate. When they arrive on board they're partially trained and we've just got a few little bits to fine tune.

Once they actually get on board it really depends on who they are – whether they're brand new or whether they're existing employees coming back.

In the past everyone got exactly the same training but now we're prioritising our training and focusing on what we need to deliver.

Crewmembers meet with one of the fleet trainers – we've got trainers on all our ships, all very approachable guys – and we'll do a small induction on board. One of the first tasks will be to check the assessment, to make sure it was actually the crewmember that did it, that they didn't do it three weeks ago and have maybe forgotten everything. We want to check they've still got the knowledge base in there.

One of the things we can't do in the CBT is be very ship specific. We have a number of types of ships so we do need to go over some of the differences in the fire equipment, in the numbers and types of lifesaving appliances and in the general layout on board.

One of the drawbacks that we have on the ships is that they are primarily designed to put passengers in. We'd like to have a training room but we're left with wherever we can find to try and deliver training – in an unused restaurant, mid-service; in a small crew room; I've even delivered training in a cabin – luckily it was a big ship and a very luxurious cabin but you don't get that many people in.

In the past we'd take hundreds of people into the theatre, they'd sit there for an hour and we would deliver a lecture. Nice comfortable seats, dim lighting and we'd just lecture away and at the end say 'Do you understand everything?' You'd get a nod or the sound of snoring from the back and that was us done. We'd ticked the box.

Now we've streamlined the numbers and we're targeting people properly. It's easier to take, say, 12 cabin stewards away than it was to take a hundred or more because we're really not affecting their service that much. Now the trainer can deliver at a pace the learner needs. We feel that we've got it right and they're really going away with something useful.

Because we can only deliver training at certain times, we've got plenty of time in which to follow up. When the fleet trainers are not training they'll be out and about, either delivering toolbox talks or just general Q&A sessions. In the past we've used a lot of manuals but nobody likes flicking through a book trying to find anything. Now it's all on computer, which makes things a lot, lot simpler for people.

Andy Parkin - Account Lead – Defence & Maritime, ONE TWO FOUR

OneTwoFour has been working with Carnival for about two and a half years now and we're focused on helping them deliver a blended learning package across a number of subjects. The initial requirement was for a health and safety programme but it wasn't just about e-learning, it was about providing them with media-rich learning experiences, led by a very strong instructional design component.

Joanna Kori, Learning Consultant

We carried out quite a bit of research. I went on board ship; I spoke to a lot of trainers; I observed a number of different situations in which they were training. As a qualified teacher I was actually full of admiration for the flexibility the fleet trainers had in adapting to all different types of situations – they had to be quite inventive. I felt it was really important to give them a chance to train in a way that would really make use of their skills and abilities, which wasn't happening.

Carnival really wanted a solution that was contemporary and exciting. A lot of their audience was very used to mobile phones and computers to communicate back home or to improve themselves, so I knew that there needed to be a digital element.

We were aware of new approaches to teaching coming in, in particular the 'flipped classroom'.

Instead of information delivery happening in the classroom and people then going away and applying that knowledge as 'homework', people gain their information outside of the classroom; then, when they get together with the teacher, the emphasis is on application. This takes teachers away from their role of being the 'sage on the stage', giving the learner the responsibility for acquiring new knowledge at their own pace, and providing a new responsibility for the teacher as a 'guide on the side'.

Andy

We've developed a virtual fire extinguisher, which can be deployed on board and which coaches the teams in effective fire control.

Imagine there's a carbonaceous fire started from a waste paper bin in a cabin. The user is encouraged, using a Wii controller, to identify where that fire is, extinguish it and make the correct emergency responses. The first thing the user is required to do is raise the alarm. Then they investigate the fire and select the most appropriate appliance to fight it.

With a carbonaceous fire we're going to select a foam fire extinguisher – if you put a water fire extinguisher on an electrical fire then you would see

sparks and the user would get a shudder through the controller to indicate that they were being electrocuted. With the fire now out, the user can to take the final action, which is to evacuate the compartment.

Jo

We looked at ways in which we could take people to environments on the ship – say the watertight doors – and we'd be pressing buttons, we'd be looking at what actually happens, there'd maybe be a slightly gory description of what would be the result if you got trapped in one, and people would be actively trying the things out. This was a much more satisfactory learning experience for everybody.

We piloted the initial design of the e-learning with all the fleet trainers as part of an annual workshop. We captured a lot of their initial responses, which were, in the main, really positive but they also had some fantastic suggestions for ways in which the e-learning could be designed to be complementary to the follow-up training.

They were also very interested in using some new teaching and training techniques which a lot of them hadn't had the chance to try before. It became a really fantastic group design.

We went from an e-learning solution to a very Carnival UK blended learning programme and, because of that, so many people have embraced it as something that's quite special to them and special to Carnival as well.

John

The new induction programme is hugely successful, both for the business and the crewmember. For the crewmember it means they can do training in their own time and use the content as an aide memoire. We're also able to deliver the training before people board the ship. It provides them with a broad knowledge of the experience they'll have when they get on the ship for the first time.

For the business, we've managed to take some of the training materials we were delivering using a 'sheep dip' approach and make it much more targeted. We've been able to extend the time between the repeat training that we do on board. For some subjects, such as Watertight Doors, we were training every three months but we've been able to extend that now to a 12-month period, because we can assess their competence more readily.

ANALYSED: CREW TRAINING AT CARNIVAL UK

The situation

The need	The primary need was for a more effective induction programme for crewmembers. With the previous programme, all the training was concentrated in a short period with everyone receiving the same training, regardless of need.
The learning	The requirement is for crewmembers to know the relevant health and safety and security procedures and be able to apply them in practice. Above all, they needed to support and contribute to an overall culture of safety.
The learners	There are as many as 2,000 crewmembers joining a ship. They come from across the world and therefore English will often be a second language. The training is applicable to all levels on board a ship.
The logistics	When on board, Internet connectivity is patchy and there are no dedicated training facilities. In addition, little time is available for training.

The blend

	Methods	*Media*
Preparation	As part of the recruitment process, information is gathered about crewmembers' core skills and experience.	Face to face
	Each new crewmember is provided with access to a suite of interactive learning materials and an assessment that must be successfully completed before joining.	Online materials
	Once on board, a further check is made that the crewmember has the requisite knowledge.	Face-to-face contact with on-board fleet trainer
Input	Depending on role and experience, crewmembers attend a short induction, as well as receiving ship-specific training.	Face-to-face with the fleet trainer
Application	Depending on role and experience, crewmembers get to visit key sites, such as the watertight doors.	Face to face
	Simulations are available to allow further practice of safety procedures, such as using fire extinguishers.	Interactive computer simulation used in face-to-face sessions
Follow-up	Fleet trainers provide informal talks and Q&A sessions as needed.	Face to face
	Reference materials are available as needed.	Online

PART 4
STRUCTURE

STRUCT—URING

S

TURIN

TRUCT
G YOUR BLEND

FOUR PHASES
IN AN EFFECTIVE BLEND

It is somewhat surprising to find myself reflecting on the work of a French singer in a book on blended learning. It's true that, at the time the idea originally came to me, I was on my way to Lyon to run a workshop on blended learning, but the connection was and is tenuous to say the least.

As I made my way to France, I had been refining my ideas for the design of blended solutions for close to ten years, testing them against hundreds of different real-world problems. I felt comfortable with the processes I had settled on for gathering data about the requirements of a particular situation, and for the way in which decisions were made about methods and media.

But until that point in time I had thought it unlikely that you could follow a standard sequence within blended solutions, a series of phases that could be applied effectively in a wide variety of situations. However, what I found when I looked back over many different designs was that successful solutions seemed to follow a certain pattern of four phases. I struggled to find names for these phases that would apply to both formal and non-formal interventions using a wide range of different strategies, but I was happy with what I settled on. As you can imagine, I was amused when the initial letters of the four phases spelled out the name PIAF.

Here are the phases:

Preparation: In this phase your aim is to prepare the learner for a productive learning experience, and to make sure anyone involved in providing the solution is geared up to meet the needs of the particular learner. In this phase you may include measures to pinpoint areas of need, establish goals, address any shortcomings in prerequisite knowledge, introduce learners to each other and to the tools and equipment they will be using, and provide an overview of what is to follow.

Input: This phase represents the primary formal element of the programme. This is when your learners participate in activities like workshops, on-job instruction or webinars, or when they engage with the core learning materials.

Application: In this phase, learners put what they have learned into action, whether directly on the job or through individual and group assignments. With larger programmes, Input and Application are likely to cycle as the learner progresses through a number of modules.

Follow-up: It is very unlikely that you will have achieved your objectives fully at the end of the Application phase.

The Follow-up phase allows your solution to become an on-going process rather than a one-off event.

You will look to provide facilities such as coaching and materials that the learner can access on demand. As the balance shifts from 'courses' to 'resources', the Follow-up phase will become increasingly dominant.

PIAF is not rocket science. I'm sure that, given the chance, you'd have come up with something similar – but that does not mean it is common sense. Most learning interventions have just one phase – Input, typically a classroom course or a piece of e-learning. They are disconnected from the real world in which the employee operates. They struggle to make an impact, even when – at the time – they are engaging and enjoyable.

What PIAF does is to put formal Input in its place – just one step in an on-going learner journey that will most likely also include non-formal, on-demand and experiential elements.

BLENDING IN

PIAF is helpful because it does not unduly focus on the Input phase; it blends this into a process that starts and ends in the real work environment. So, why is 'blending in' so important?

Preparation: Any sort of formal input – from a series of virtual classroom sessions, to an online simulation, to the meeting of an action learning set – needs a clear purpose. In the Preparation phase, the learner, ideally in partnership with their manager, can reflect on their needs and establish goals. If there is any misalignment between the upcoming Input and the learner's starting point then this can be addressed here: the Input can be adapted to better meet the learner's needs; the learner can undertake some preliminary study to make sure they are fully prepared to take advantage of the Input; elements of Input that are not relevant to the learner can be removed. As a result, the Input phase will *blend in* more effectively – it will not be isolated or misaligned.

Preparation has another important role, which is to begin addressing the learner's hopes and fears – their emotional response to the intervention. While a focus on performance is important, it is not sufficient. The Preparation phase can be used to build relationships between peers, to establish ground rules, to address concerns and to align the intervention with the learner's personal aspirations.

Application: Without Application, all we are left with is good intentions – skills remain rudimentary and ideas untested. Application is when you should start to get a return on the investment that has been made in Input; 'should' because sometimes the skills you have started to develop and the ideas you have provisionally taken on board will not deliver on the promise and will fail to improve your performance; but without Application you will never know.

Follow-up: An intervention is just that; it is an interlude on the journey, not the journey itself. The Follow-up phase embeds the learning into the everyday job environment, helping the learner to refine their skills and ideas and to keep up-to-date with the continually changing demands of the job. This phase sees a shift from push to pull, and from courses to resources. As their confidence increases, the employee will start to become an actor in supporting others, a teacher as well as a learner. This phase is also the point at which all other interventions, such as rewards and recognition programmes, changes to supervision, investments in new systems, equipment and so on, combine with the learning to reach the goal.

WHY WE NEED BOTH COURSES AND RESOURCES

Courses have, historically, been what L&D does, perhaps even its *raison d'être*. And courses will continue to play an important role, particularly with novices who 'don't know what they don't know' and when formal confirmation is required that particular learning objectives have been achieved. Courses may take place in a classroom, online, on-job or by some blend of these, but they all typically have objectives, entry criteria, a curriculum, formal content, tuition and assessment. More often than not they also take place at a predetermined time and are 'pushed' at a particular population. All of this structure helps an organisation to make sure that certain key interventions do take place in the intended fashion, but does not guarantee success. All too often, courses fail to fulfil their aims:

- They are frequently forced on those who don't need them.

- Timing is rarely ideal – often they are too early or too late.

- They are often knowledge-focused and, as a result, serve only to overwhelm the learner with new information, without placing this in context.

- They typically provide nowhere near enough opportunities for practice and feedback.

- They can include invalid or unreliable assessments, which lull the employer and the learner into a false sense of security[11].

- They make little provision for follow-up once the course has been completed.

11_ *My colleague Phil Green suggests the example of an airline pilot who achieves 90% in his assessment. We should worry if the other 10% includes how to land the plane.*

There's nothing wrong with courses as such, it's just that we place too much attention on them and not enough on what happens afterwards. By and large, we would do well to teach much less and provide much more in the way of support. Courses are for stories, scenarios, simulations and discussions; resources are where you go to find the information you need to follow up on your interest. These resources can take many forms:

- Experts that we can call upon for information.

- Coaches who can help us to analyse our successes and failures and establish our goals.

- Colleagues who share our interests and can respond to our requests for assistance.

- Packaged content that can provide us with information and help in diagnosing problems and making decisions. These can include checklists, aides-memoires, decision aids, posters, templates and expert systems.

- Forums and other collaborative tools that allow us to share expertise and solve problems.

- The learner's own notes.

The argument for shifting the emphasis from teaching everything formally up front to teaching the essentials and then providing other information on demand has strengthened over the past few years:

- We now have a much better understanding of how easy it is to overwhelm learners, particularly novices, with information and how little of this information is retained.

- The easy availability of information through search engines and on mobile devices makes it much more practical to provide resources as and when needed.

- Expectations have changed. Employees no longer expect to have to learn large quantities of information up front, when it can so easily be made available on demand.

ACHIEVING UNCONSCIOUS COMPETENCE

I must admit I used to think of that widely known, four-step process that sees a learner move from unconscious incompetence through conscious incompetence to conscious competence and finally unconscious competence as an amusing play on words and not much more. But I have started to find

it quite useful as a way of explaining the learner's journey as they develop new skills, and it fits snugly with the concept of courses and resources, in itself my favourite way of explaining the relationship between formal and informal learning.

In case you haven't encountered the four steps before, the idea is that the learner starts in a state of unconscious incompetence with regard to a new area of skill. They don't know what they don't know. The skill looks straightforward enough. There's probably not a lot to it.

Of course, when they do get to have a go, they find it's a lot harder than they thought. They don't have any of the elaborate schemas built up by expert performers over time and they flounder. They graduate to a state of conscious incompetence – they now know that they don't know. At this point, some learners will turn and run but, assuming the skill is worth having, most will be highly motivated to learn.

Repeated practice with supportive feedback will bring those that persevere to a state of conscious competence. They can perform the skill – just – but because the elements of the skill are still not sufficiently drilled in, their working memory is overloaded with 'things they must not forget to do' and they're struggling to hold it all together.

The reward comes in time. Eventually the skill becomes so deeply embedded that they are hardly aware of what they are doing. They may even be able to carry out the skill in the background, leaving their working memory free to cope with the unexpected or to carry out another task altogether. This is unconscious competence.

So how do courses and resources fit into this? According to Nick Shackleton-Jones's model, the course (which we can regard as any more or less formal learning intervention) has two purposes: (1) to inspire the learner, to have them care about what needs to be learned, to arouse the emotions, and (2) to instil the learner with sufficient confidence that they will be able to continue their learning journey independently.

So how do these map to the four steps? Well, one of the ways that you generate an emotional reaction is by demonstrating that there really is a learning need. You want the learner to be thinking, 'This stuff seems to matter. I should probably know how to do it but I don't.' In other words, the learner is consciously incompetent. That's what any skill-building course

should accomplish early on but so many don't. If you haven't put the learner in a situation where their lack of skill becomes obvious to them, then they won't realise. You have to let them have a go.

Starting a course with a load of theory isn't going to demonstrate need.

It is far better to engage the learner in a practical activity (a case study, scenario, group challenge, simulation, etc.) that puts their skill (or lack of it) to the test – safely, of course, and without embarrassment. When they become frustrated by obstacles to their progress then, believe me, they'll be willing to learn.

Most skill-building courses, even those that devote too long to the theory, will provide some practice. The trouble is that this is often limited to one or two brief attempts – just enough for the learner to be conscious of their incompetence. This is not a happy state in which to end a course – in a way, the learner is worse off than when they started.

When you're learning any new skill, you need plenty of safe practice. Mistakes should be encouraged, even welcomed; nobody gets hurt and nobody is out of pocket.

And ideally, no-one is trying to impress their peers, just to develop their skills.

Most courses end with the learner in a state of conscious incompetence, but if the aim of the course really is to instil confidence, then it needs to get the learner well on the path to conscious competence – perhaps not all the way there, but confident enough to progress more independently. Only with confidence can the learner move on from the course to take advantage of the resources, whether these are in the form of content, or support from a coach, buddy, mentor, supervisor or peers.

WHY YOU DON'T *ALWAYS* NEED A COURSE

More and more, we are being asked by clients to help them assemble a collection of resources to support some new business initiative. Not courses – although they may also provide some of these – but resources. These resources are not 'pushed' at people, who have to use them whether they like it or not; they are 'pulled' as and when needed. They don't sit on a learning management system (LMS), where each individual's usage is monitored, but on the intranet or the wider Internet, where they can be freely accessed at any time and found using a search engine.

These resources can take various forms:

- Web articles, written in an engaging, journalistic manner, rather like blog posts.

- More formal reference material, in HTML or PDF format.

- Decision aids, perhaps coded in Flash or JavaScript, but sometimes more simply provided as spreadsheets, tables or diagrams.

- Self-analysis questionnaires or perhaps quizzes.

- Short, simple videos and screencasts.

- Advance organisers, mind-maps or quick reference guides.

- Mini-scenarios that allow the user to check whether they can put what they have learned into practice.

Sometimes the things that make the biggest difference can be very low-tech, perhaps a 'smile before you dial' sticker on a call-handler's phone or numbers and arrows which show the safe start-up and close-down or maintenance of a machine.

Resources like these are flexible because elements can be added, removed and edited at any time, whether that's because the subject matter itself has changed or in response to user feedback. For each element, you can select the best tool for development and the most flexible format for delivery. You can develop the simple ones yourself and bring in help to produce more sophisticated elements where necessary. Importantly, you can go live as soon as the first few elements are ready – there's no reason to wait until the whole collection is finished.

In many cases, users will find the resources they want using the intranet's search function, but you can help users by providing some additional form of curation. Perhaps the best way is to create gateway pages, which provide links to the most useful resources around a particular topic, in a logical sequence and with clear indications of just who is likely to benefit. In one project I used web articles as the gateways, each article drawing on the resources most closely related to the particular topic.

I've come to realise for myself just how useful this approach can be. A few years ago I spent far too much money on a Canon 5D Mark III, a professional stills and HD video camera, with a whole load of complex accessories. It would have been unforgivable not to take full advantage of the opportunities that such a sophisticated camera provided, so I set about getting myself genned up. Here is what I collected in the first few weeks:

- Two iPad apps which provided video 'lessons', one for the particular model of camera and one on DSLR photography/videography in general.

- Endless YouTube videos.

- A number of popular blogs that I have subscribed to and continue to read.

- A couple of digital arts/photography magazines on the Apple Newsstand.

Would I also take a course? Possibly yes, perhaps even a face-to-face one with real people in a real local college (although a collaborative online course would probably also work well). But I wouldn't depend on this, because no course is going to provide exactly what I want when I want it. The how-to information I can find for myself, as I need it.

The application of this knowledge is another matter. Ideally you need feedback on your own work and to provide feedback to others; you need to share perspectives with others in your position and draw on the wisdom of experts. Courses and resources – we may differ in the extent to which we need each of these, but ultimately we need them both.

LEARNERS CAN PIAF FOR THEMSELVES

In a situation in which there is no course, just resources, it would be easy to see this as a situation in which PIAF breaks down – we are left with the F.

But learners can – and frequently do – manage the learning process just as thoroughly on their own.

Here's how PIAF works when the learner is the principal actor in the learning process, not a professional teacher:

Preparation: Learners can figure out for themselves what they need to know or what they must be able to do and how they should progress with accomplishing their goal. Of course you could provide a resource to help them figure this out – perhaps a diagnostic questionnaire.

Input: Learners can hunt down the resources they need to provide the core knowledge and skills needed to achieve their goal, just as I did when I bought my new camera. And again, you could help by picking out the most useful resources and providing learners with suggestions.

Application: The same goes for this phase. Many learners will be dying to try out their new knowledge and skills and will make this happen as a priority. If they are unsure how to get started, you can suggest activities that have worked well for others.

Follow-up: As learners progress on their journey, they can hunt down additional resources on the Internet or from their own circle of contacts. If necessary, you can help in your role as 'curator'.

Psychologists call the ability to recognise your own learning needs and determine a strategy to address these needs *metacognitive skills*. Some of us will currently have more of these skills than others, but there is evidence to suggest that these skills can be developed over time.

It is just possible that, as more and more people discover how easy it is to learn independently using the Internet, they will become more confident as learners. In terms of their metacognitive skills, they will move to a state of conscious competence and ultimately unconscious competence. In this happy state, they are likely to pronounce that they don't need courses any more, believing that their newfound skills are just common sense and common practice. They are not.

ALIGNING THE LEARNER AND THE INTERVENTION

As we've seen, the purpose of the Preparation phase is to align the learner and the intervention – learners prepare to take full advantage of the intervention, and the intervention is adjusted to the needs of learners.

Why is this necessary? Let's look first of all at the ways in which the learner may not be aligned with the intervention.

Potential misalignment	What you could do about it
The learner is not motivated to participate / they do not see the point	This will happen quite regularly with mandated courses, particularly those that an organisation needs to provide to meet the requirements of a regulatory authority or to ensure compliance with an important policy. There is little point in driving on with the course if the learner is not motivated. You have to start by making clear why the intervention is important, not just to the organisation, but to the learner. Doing this in an authoritarian way will not help one bit. With a little imagination, perhaps some storytelling, you can contrive a situation in which the need for the intervention becomes self-evident, another example of the power of guided discovery as a strategy.

Potential misalignment	What you could do about it
The learner does not have the prerequisite knowledge	If you move ahead with the intervention without addressing this, you will have some stressed out participants. Those learners without the necessary knowledge will be anxious because they will find it hard to keep up; those who did meet the requirements will be angry that their time is being wasted going back to material they have already covered.
	You can, of course, turn away learners who do not have the prerequisite knowledge. On the other hand, in the Preparation phase, you could provide materials that help those without the necessary knowledge to get up to speed before the Input phase starts.
The learner does not know what the intervention will entail (objectives, process, hardware and software requirements, etc.)	A clear overview of the intervention will help the learner to prepare psychologically for what is to follow. This is often called an advance organiser[13]; it helps the learner to see how each piece of input fits in and how it relates to their past experience.
	A description of the hardware and software requirements is essential for any intervention that uses technology and is easily included in the overview of the intervention.
	A clear overview of the intervention will help the learner to prepare psychologically for what is to follow. This is often called an advance organiser[13]; it helps the learner to see how each piece of input fits in and how it relates to their past experience.
	A description of the hardware and software requirements is essential for any intervention that uses technology and is easily included in the overview of the intervention.

Potential misalignment	What you could do about it
The learner is not clear what his/her own goals are	Clarification of the learner's goals is important for a number of reasons. Firstly, it helps the learner to focus on the activities and resources that will most benefit them. Secondly, it will help other learners to see where they have opportunities to help out. Thirdly, it may be that the intervention can be tweaked to ensure that the learner's goals are adequately addressed. It can be useful to include an activity that requires the learner to have a conversation with their supervisor or manager. This will ensure the learner's goals are aligned with the goals of the wider department and that the supervisor or manager is fully behind the learner as they progress through the intervention.
The learner is apprehensive about the intervention	Anxiety is not conducive to learning, so it is important to address any concerns as part of the Preparation phase. Perhaps the best strategy is to provide plenty of information about the intervention, particularly in those areas which might give cause for concern, e.g. how learning will be assessed, the types of activities learners will be asked to engage in, who else will be participating in the intervention, how much time will be required to complete the activities, etc.

13_ 'The most important single factor influencing learning is what the learner already knows': David Ausubel.

Potential misalignment	What you could do about it
The learner is unfamiliar with the other participants	Another way to reduce anxiety is to introduce the learner to their fellow participants as early as possible. Learners will be particularly looking for others who share the same goals, have similar experience or could possibly help them to achieve their goals. In an online course, this function can be achieved by asking learners to create and share an online profile and then allow participants to make contact with each other, perhaps using a forum. Another option is to hold a welcome session, face to face or online, in which participants can introduce each other.

Now let's look at the ways in which the intervention may not be aligned with its participants. If there is a misalignment, you can, of course, simply direct the learner towards another, more suitable, intervention, should one exist. However, it may be possible for some aspects of an intervention to be shaped around its particular audience.

Potential misalignment	What you could do about it
The intervention may be pitched at too high or low a level for the participants	Facilitators can be alerted to the potential problem and make a special effort to address the needs of those for whom the intervention would otherwise be pitched too high or low. It may be possible for extra modules to be added or removed from the programme for selected participants. The level at which learners enter the intervention may also be taken into account in the selection of participants for groups.
The intervention may not be directly relevant to the participants	The obvious action here is to include additional examples that are more relevant.
The intervention may not be convenient to participants in terms of dates, times, locations, etc.	Perhaps an adjustment can be made to any of these parameters to better suit the participants. Perhaps some live sessions can be run online to reduce travel difficulties. These sessions could be run at more than one time of day if there is a problem with time zones.

A LITTLE INPUT GOES A LONG WAY

For longer interventions, in which there is a substantial amount of material to cover, a simple Preparation-Input-Application-Follow-up sequence is not going to work. As a general rule, learners want to get on with applying what they have learned as soon as possible. If there is too much Input before Application, learners will become stressed about the amount they have to remember, and inevitably much that is important will be forgotten.

A few years ago I was meeting with a learning and development team and we were discussing principles upon which we could base the design of future programmes. One of the team suggested the following:

Provide only as much information as the learner must have in order to start practising and no more.

I took this principle to heart and have tried hard ever since to apply it in my own designs. Really it is common sense, but very rarely applied in a corporate context. Outside of work you would take it for granted. Imagine you signed up for a tennis lesson. The coach spent

50 minutes describing the history of the game, the different strokes, the rules and the tactics. He or she then suggested you have a go for the last ten minutes. Would you return for another lesson? Of course not.

If you do have a lot of material to cover, you have two possible solutions. The first is to keep the Input phase to a minimum and then feed in additional information through the feedback that you provide in the Application phase and the additional resources you offer during Follow-up.

Your second option is to loop Input and Application: provide some Input, then Application, then some more Input, some more Application and so on. You could call this process PIAIAIAF, but it wouldn't be so memorable. Essentially what you have done is to break your intervention up into modules or perhaps weekly/monthly classes.

APPLYING PIAF IN A VARIETY OF DIFFERENT CONTEXTS

PIAF is a simple, yet versatile process, which can be applied in a variety of contexts. Hopefully the following table will provide you with some ideas for ways in which PIAF can be applied to the sorts of interventions for which you are responsible. In each case, these are just examples of what can be done, not universal formulae.

	Preparation	*Input*	*Application*	*Follow-up*
Skills-based training in the workplace	Diagnostic skills assessment; overview of the intervention.	Instruction, including demonstrations; Q&A.	Opportunities to practise with feedback, starting off-job and gradually moving on-job. <<< loop as necessary	On-going access to performance support materials and coaching.
Knowledge-based course in the workplace	Diagnostic knowledge assessment, background study.	Self-paced materials; Q&A.	Opportunities for regular rehearsal and application of the knowledge. <<< loop as necessary	On-going access to performance support materials and further exploration of the domain.
Ideas-based course in the workplace	Goal setting, surveys; background study; meeting the cohort.	Group activities and discussion; individual study.	Work-based projects and assignments. <<< loop as necessary	Reviewing goals; surveys; exploring resources; sharing experiences.
Coaching relationship	Forming the coaching relationship; establishing overall goals.	Coaching sessions to reflect on progress and agree new actions.	The coachee works on the agreed actions. <<< loop as necessaryy	Periodic follow-up.
Action learning set	Forming the set; establishing goals.	Meetings of the action learning set.	Progressing the projects. <<< loop as necessary	Evaluating learning; keeping up-to-date on project results.

	Preparation	*Input*	*Application*	*Follow-up*
Full-time vocational college course	Diagnostic assessments; background study.	Classroom sessions; self-study materials.	Projects and assignments; possible work placements. <<< loop as necessary	Careers planning, suggestions for further learning, alumni groups.
Part-time vocational college course	Diagnostic assessment; meeting fellow learners; background study.	Release from work to attend classes; live online sessions; self-study materials.	Practical assignments, ideally work-related; work experience. <<< loop as necessary	Suggestions for further learning; alumni groups.
Public short course run by a training provider	Diagnostic questionnaire; introductory live online session; background study.	Classroom session / workshop.	Practical assignments, ideally work-related; work experience; live online session to review progress.	Suggestions for further learning; alumni groups.
A learner-led solution using open resources / no curation	The learner identifies a need and resolves to address it.	The learner hunts down resources that meet their need for knowledge.	The learner endeavours to put what they have learned into practice.	The learner tops up their knowledge as needed using open resources.
A curated learner-led solution using open resources	Diagnostic questionnaire / assessment.	Suggested resources providing knowledge and information.	Suggested activities for putting the learning into practice / feedback from peers.	Suggested resources for further exploration.

THE

BL

COLLECTION:

HC-ONE

HC-ONE

FEELS
THE
POWER

This case study shows how a richly blended solution, expertly implemented, can contribute to a major business turn-around, in this case within the care sector. HC-One, working with partners Acteon, achieved all this within a year of go-ahead. Here's how.

TALKING ABOUT TOUCH

Alison Innes-Farquhar, Head of People and Organisational Development, HC-One

HC-One is a new company formed out of the rescue of a care home group called Southern Cross, back in November, 2011. HC-One is a group of 220 care homes, from literally the Isle of Sky to Belfast, Southampton to Swansea – so right across four different principalities, involving four different regulators. We care for 10,500 residents, many of whom are living with dementia. We have, currently, 14,500 colleagues, delivering or supporting the care of residents within the care homes.

This was a fascinating project.

> We inherited a disillusioned and disengaged workforce. We had somehow to reach them, to be able to transform the way that they worked.

Our principle concern was and remains, the care of residents. They had to be safe and happy, and we knew we could only do this by delivering the kindest care. That meant having a workforce that was competent, confident, and compliant, and that's what drove this programme right from day one.

Our first and most important priority was to have a compliant workforce, so, all the mandatory training that each of the regulators required of us. That's where we started, and we put all our energy into delivering that programme, first of all face to face, and then we put much of the material online. We wanted to build something that was fun and yet meaningful, and that people really wanted to do. It's unusual for people to want to do health and safety training, but we made it interesting and fun, so that they chose to do it as opposed to being told to do it.

We have such a mix of people, from maintenance operatives to housekeepers, catering assistants, carers, nurses, clinical leads, home managers and administrators. So of course, that attracts a number of different types of people, but all of them are 'people people'. They want to spend their time with their colleagues and with the older people that we care for. So they're not necessarily the sort of people who'd want to sit down at a computer or go sit in a classroom.

There were naturally a number of constraints in developing and rolling out this programme, particularly around things like geography. There were no networks in the care homes, so we had to put them all in. That meant taking down ceilings and walls in people's homes. That was difficult, especially when it was a couple of hundred miles away, and you were relying on contractors to do the work for you.

We had time constraints too. We launched HC-One in November 2011, and we promised that we would deliver this programme by September 2012. So we had ten months to network a whole group of care homes and to develop the bespoke programme, and run workshops and road shows as part of the communication plan. It was tough but we had a great team who believed in what we were doing.

We required a certain amount of change management with this programme having inherited such a disengaged workforce. They were resistant to even more change, and they put up lots of barriers. We expected that; the usual: "I've never used a computer. I like to

be with the residents all the time, not sitting in a classroom." So we worked through those, and we managed to break those barriers down slowly by using stories from the pilot.

One of the most important things that we did to introduce the programme to all colleagues in the group was to have a really strong communication plan. We literally 'drip-fed' little pieces of information to the group, building up anticipation of what was to come We also created an identity, which has stuck absolutely through everything that we do, and that's the identity of *Touch*.

Touch is a fully blended learning programme. We have a number of different ways in which we deliver content. We have face-to-face workshops, of course, and traditional e-learning. We've also shot a number of videos using our own people with residents, all very short, showing a practice or a procedure. We have short animations, which get over key points with the aid of music.

We've created games for people to play, even sometimes with residents. We have a number of what we call 'spark cards'. This is where someone might have a few minutes with colleagues, waiting for something to happen, like a lunch

trolley to arrive, and they will debate a subject that's on the card. So they say, 'Well, if it was Edith who had this problem, what would we do?' It's brilliant, because is makes people think, yet there is no right or wrong answer

We also gave all our learning and development facilitators flip cameras and audio recorders, so they could make their own podcasts and little video clips of something that they've captured when they're in the homes. So peers contribute to their own learning, and they love it.

Another part of the blend is something that we term 'offline activities', in which we ask people to demonstrate what it is that they have learned, say putting someone in the recovery position. Now, watching it on an e-learning module doesn't mean that they know how to do it, so we get them to practise it and someone who's supervising them signs it off. It's about being competent, not just having knowledge.

It's so important to keep learning alive. While we require our colleagues to do refresher training, maybe every 12 months, two years, three years, you can't just leave it for all of that time.

We like to remind them about the salient points within the learning. So this is when we would use mini movies as a little reminder, to say: 'These are the most important points that you need to carry out.' We do keep it alive also with performance support tools, through spark cards and things like that, that you can use any time of the year.

We also make sure that their learning is discussed in supervision or at handover, so it's never lost; it's always on the agenda. People are always talking about, 'What if? How would I react? What do I need to know?'

The results that we've had from Touch have been absolutely incredible. In the first two years, we have run 52,000 workshops and over 400,000 online modules have been completed.

When we did an evaluation of what people thought about *Touch*, when we first launched, we had over 90% who said that they loved it. Now, that is brilliant. We also asked them in our staff survey each year, 'What's the best thing that HC-One has done for you?' Three years running, it's been training and development, which is absolutely thrilling, especially as there is no prompt – they could have said anything.

But of course, we can't ignore the fact that we've had external acknowledgement too, with no less than eight national and international awards. We have been recognised by Camilla Cavendish in the Cavendish review of healthcare training, following the Francis Report. HC-One was highlighted as being best practice training for healthcare, and we are being used now to help design a programme for healthcare assistants in hospitals and in care homes across the country, which will be launched next year.

Dr Chai Patel, Chairman, HC-One

An organisation can have an aspiration to be whatever it is they want to be. In our case, we've taken on the pretty daunting, rather ambitious task of wanting to be the kindest care home operator in the UK. You can't achieve a goal like that without providing the best people, who we're trying to recruit, with the best skills. *Touch* is the platform with which we do that. *Touch* is a way of saying, 'We mean what we say and we're going to help you achieve that transformation'. And I think in the end, transformation only takes place when the behaviour of the whole organisation changes.

Through *Touch* we've been able to link the company's aspirations with those of the staff, and we've achieved that through competence, through skills, and allowing people to get the confidence and the belief that what they want to do, what our residents expect, and what we want to do are totally aligned.

In this blended way of learning, Touch is about giving people the skills to do their job to the best of their ability, and to give them the confidence that they are doing the very best they can do for the residents.

ANALYSED: HC-ONE'S TOUCH PROGRAMME

The situation

The need	The much-publicised demise of Southern Cross left the legacy of poor management and a disengaged and disillusioned workforce. The business needed to re-engage its staff.
The learning	HC-One was looking to increase certified compliance from 20% to 85% in 12 months, at a 50% lower cost, while increasing staff engagement by 5% (all of which were achieved). However, *Touch* had three additional objectives: 1. To move from a culture of 'training for compliance' to a culture of 'learning to deliver the kindest care'. 2. To embed learning rather than just provide it. 3. To use the most appropriate channels to meet the business need.
The learners	HC-One encompasses a very wide range of roles, but staff can be characterised as 'people people', not those likely to want to sit in a classroom or at a computer.
The logistics	Only ten months was available to network more than 200 care homes across the UK and meet the business objectives.

The blend

	Methods	Media
Preparation	HC-One created the *Touch* identity, and this runs through all aspects of the programme.	
	A comprehensive communications programme prepared staff for the launch, including a nationwide roadshow.	Fourteen separate communication channels were used
Input	Classroom workshops.	Delivered face to face in the care homes
	Self-study courses, including case studies and scenarios.	E-learning
	Video programmes, presented by and featuring HC-One staff.	Online
	Animated mini-movies – short and high impact – designed to reinforce critical attitudinal or behavioural messages and act as teasers to introduce new courses.	Online
	Peer-contributed content – audio and video.	Online

	Methods	*Media*
Application	'Spark cards', used to encourage debate.	Self-directed, face to face
	'Offline activities' that help to embed the learning. These are used as the basis for guided supervision and observation.	Face to face
Follow-up	Animated mini-movies and spark cards are used to keep the learning alive.	Various
	Learning is on the agenda in meetings with supervisors and in handovers.	Face to face
	Every home has a specially trained *Touch* learning ambassador.	

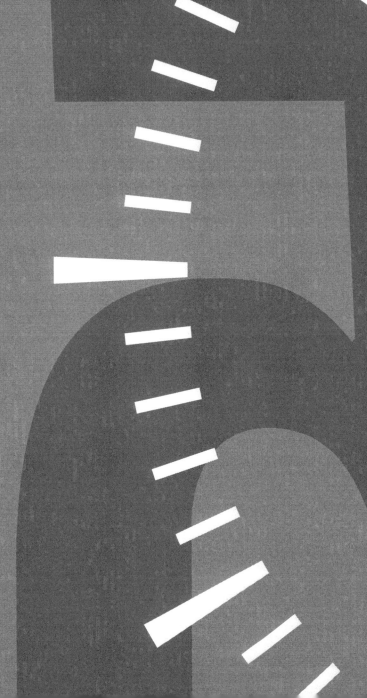

PART 5
METHODS

LEARNING METHODS ARE TIMELESS

Strange as it may seem, the methods we use for teaching and learning have been with us for a very long time. Thousands of years ago, the Greek philosopher Socrates would have had very much the same choices as you do now. If he ever became tired of Socratic questioning, the great man could have employed a wide variety of alternative approaches – lectures, games, role-plays, case studies, demonstrations, assignments, discussions, and so on. These methods may go in and out of fashion or be dressed up with fancy new names (so 'job aids' become 'performance support') but the idea stays essentially the same. As Juliet so wisely remarked: 'That which we call a rose by any other name would smell as sweet.'

Learning methods are the tools we use to facilitate learning. Importantly, they – and not technologies – are the principal determinant of whether a solution will or will not be effective[12].

That's why we have to get the methods right first. A blended solution should not involve a trade-off between effectiveness and efficiency. When following the *More Than* process, the idea is to select an effective strategy first and then – without compromise – to choose the most streamlined mode of delivery. That way, quality is a given.

So how do we select the most appropriate methods? Well, this is not entirely a rule-based process; it requires you to make careful judgements based on what you know of the particular situation and how you apply key learning principles. There are two ways in which you can systematise your decision-making and make sure that you consider all the options, rather than relying on the same old, familiar techniques. For each major element in your blend, you need to select the most appropriate options in terms of:

1. Strategy for learning (exposition, instruction, guided discovery or exploration)

2. Social context for learning (self-study, one-to-one, group or community)

In the chapters that follow, we will explore each of these two means for analysing methods in some detail. And then, in the last chapter in this section, we bring this all together in the form of a compendium of teaching and learning methods.

12_ *We examine this evidence later in the chapter 'Making the case for blended learning'.*

BLENDING BY STRATEGY FOR LEARNING

OVERVIEW

Every learning solution, formal or informal, employs one or more of the following four basic strategies, whether or not the decision to use these strategies has been made consciously:

Exposition

Exposition is the simple delivery of information from subject expert to learner. Typically this process is required as part of a formal syllabus.

Examples include lectures, presentations and prescribed reading.

The person that drives this strategy is typically the subject expert.

Instruction

With instruction, a more systematic process is applied. This process typically starts with some specific learning objectives and culminates in some form of assessment. Along the way, a variety of media may be used to convey information and all sorts of practical exercises used to help the learner develop the required knowledge and skills.

Instruction can take place in the classroom, through self-study e-learning or on the job.

The driver for this strategy is the instructor or, in the case of self-study materials, the instructional designer.

Guided discovery

Guided discovery is also a carefully structured process, but the emphasis here is on setting up activities from which the learner can gain their own insights and come to their own conclusions.

Within formal interventions, examples might include the use of scenarios, simulations, case studies and leadership tasks. This strategy can also be employed on the job, using techniques such as coaching, action learning, job enrichment and job rotation.

The driver for this strategy is the facilitator or, in the case of self-study materials, the designer.

Exploration

Exploration hands over control to the learner to make all the choices. There are no pre-defined objectives, no syllabus and no assessment.

The exploration strategy is most likely to be applied in the provision of on-demand support to the learner as they carry out their jobs, sometimes taking the form of content, sometimes through a help desk. But exploration is also the underlying strategy behind the use of social media at work – communities of practice, forums, wikis, etc. – that allow employees to support each other.

The driver for this strategy is the learner. Having said that, there is an important role for the learning and development professional as a sort of curator, someone who provides the learner with the appropriate tools and supports them in finding the right people and content.

Using the strategies

These strategies can be applied to any type of learning intervention. In some cases, different strategies can be used at different stages within a single solution, for example: the use of exposition for essential pre-reading, the use of instruction to convey important rules, the use of guided discovery to bring out key underlying principles, the use of exploration for on-going reference.

EXPOSITION

So what is it?

Exposition is the delivery of information from teacher or subject expert to learner. It's as simple as that.

Exposition is essentially a one-way process, although it may include some modest Q&A or discussion. The strategy is top-down and teacher-centred because it is the person designing and/ or delivering who determines what information is to be delivered and how (and sometimes also where and when).

How about some examples?

Exposition can take place in the context of an event, such as a lecture, a seminar or a presentation, whether face-to-face or online. It can also take the form of content, using text, images, animation, audio or video. Historically, content like this was delivered using books, tapes, TV and radio, CDs and DVDs, although it is more likely these days to be consumed online or downloaded for delivery on portable platforms such as smart phones and e-book readers.

What interaction takes place?

Exposition may include no interactivity at all, in which case the entire onus is on the learner to take advantage of the experience, perhaps by taking notes or making a deliberate attempt to follow up on what they read, see or hear. When the exposition is self-paced, through some form of packaged content, then the learner will have more opportunity to control the experience than they will in a live lecture or presentation. On the other hand, the live event provides more opportunities for interaction with the subject expert and other learners.

When should I use it?

For exposition to work as a strategy, the student must be a relatively independent learner, with a good awareness of what they do and do not know about the subject in question. Likely candidates include senior professionals, such as hospital consultants, lawyers, accountants, executives and academics, as well as specialists and enthusiasts in a wide range of other fields. They will be able to determine what is most relevant and therefore most important to focus on and process further, whereas the dependent or novice learner could easily be overwhelmed by the sheer volume of undifferentiated information.

Any tips?

Because of the absence of interaction, exposition requires less design than, say, highly participative face-to-face workshops and self-paced tutorials. However, careful planning is still going to be a great help to the reader, listener or viewer:

* making clear what is the most important information and what is just nice to know;

* using storytelling and anecdotes to bring abstract concepts to life;

* making the most appropriate use of media elements – text, images, animation, audio and video;

* paring down the volume of content to reduce wasted time and minimise the risk of overload;

* modularising the content so it can be easily random-accessed and reviewed.

In summary

Choose exposition as a strategy when you need to control what information is delivered and to whom, and when you feel confident that the target audience will happily be able to work with this information without a great deal of support. If you judge the situation right, then you'll save an awful lot of money by not having to run workshops or create interactive online materials.

INSTRUCTION

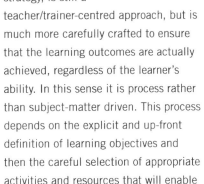

So what is it?

Instruction, the second strategy, is still a teacher/trainer-centred approach, but is much more carefully crafted to ensure that the learning outcomes are actually achieved, regardless of the learner's ability. In this sense it is process rather than subject-matter driven. This process depends on the explicit and up-front definition of learning objectives and then the careful selection of appropriate activities and resources that will enable those objectives to be achieved.

The process of 'instructional design' is teacher/trainer-centred because it focuses on learning objectives rather than learner goals; on the other hand, the fact that instruction is typically an interactive rather than a passive learner experience, means that the process can to some extent be adaptive to the individual differences of particular learners.

How about some examples?

Instruction can be a live experience, whether in the workplace ('on-job training') or in a physical or virtual classroom; it can also be self-paced, through interactive materials delivered online or using offline media (workbooks, CDs, etc.).

What interaction takes place?

Instruction is essentially interactive, whether that interaction is with content or with an instructor.

At the very least, this interaction should provide the opportunity for the learner to try things out and get personalised feedback. Ideally it will also include the ability for the learner to ask and obtain answers to questions, and to control to some extent what they learn, when and in what way.

When should I use it?

Perhaps strangely, one of the key skills for instructional designers is to recognise when instruction is and is not an appropriate strategy to use at a particular point in an intervention. You're likely to be safe going the instructional route when your target population consists of less confident learners, particularly those who are novices in the field in question, who need or want to be led step-by-step through the learning process, knowing they are capably supported. When these conditions are not met, instruction may still work, but you run the risk of 'over-teaching' and even patronising your population. Best to reserve your efforts for those who need them most.

Any tips?

While adult learning occurs in many different ways, it would be fair to say that, for most workplace trainers and e-learning designers, formal instruction is what they do. Hopefully they will be doing it well, and that means the following:

- being clear about outcomes;

- concentrating on meeting a small number of key learning objectives thoroughly, rather than covering a large number superficially;

- following an instructional process which is appropriate for the objectives in question;

- engaging the learner;

- helping the learner to make new connections with prior knowledge;

- presenting new material clearly and at an appropriate level, making use of demonstrations, stories, examples, visual aids and other tools to aid comprehension;

- providing activities that allow new knowledge and understanding to be reinforced and consolidated;

- allowing for plentiful opportunities for new skills to be practised, with the aid of timely and constructive feedback;

- being responsive to the needs of individual learners;
- providing support until all objectives are achieved.

In summary

Instruction is the most common strategy used for formal courses in the workplace. It provides the most predictable outcomes of all four strategies and is well suited to the development of skills and 'must-have' knowledge. Ideal candidates for instruction are beginners and other dependent learners who want all the support available.

GUIDED DISCOVERY

So what is it?
The third strategy, guided discovery, has many similarities with instruction in that it is very much a structured and facilitated process, but it follows a very different sequence of events.

While instruction moves from theory to practice, from the general to the specific, guided discovery starts with the specific and moves to the general.

It is an *inductive* process – it leads the learner towards insights and generalisations, rather than providing them on a plate. Because this process is much less certain and predictable, guided discovery rarely has specific learning objectives – every learner will take out of the process something unique and personal. What they take out will depend not only on the insights they gain from the particular learning experience, but also to a great deal on their prior knowledge and previous life experience.

How about some examples?
Guided discovery can take many forms – experiments in a laboratory, simulations, scenarios, case studies or team-building activities. In each of these cases, the learner is presented, alone or in a group, with a task to accomplish. Having undertaken that task, the learner or group is then encouraged to reflect on the experience – what went well, what less well? How could the successes be repeated and the failures avoided? The conclusions can be taken forward to further exercises and then hopefully applied to real-world tasks.

Guided discovery can also take place in a more informal, on-job setting. A good example is coaching. The coach helps the learner to reflect on their real-world experiences, gain insights and make new generalisations that can be tested out on future tasks. The coach's job is not so much to give advice but to challenge, support and encourage the learner as they come to their own conclusions. Job rotation and job enrichment, both of which seek to provide the employee with new job challenges, can also be regarded as examples of guided discovery.

What interaction takes place?
Like instruction, guided discovery is essentially interactive – the strategy depends on the learner being able to engage in a practical task and to obtain feedback on their decisions. The potential for meaningful insights will also be increased when there are opportunities for the learner to share perspectives with their peers.

When should I use it?
Less confident, dependent learners should be comfortable with guided discovery, as long as the process is carefully structured and facilitated, and does not leave them floundering. What is more important is that the learner should have enough knowledge and experience of the subject matter or the situations underlying the learning activity that they can make a reasonable attempt at completing the task – you

can't build on prior knowledge if you don't have any.

Guided discovery really delivers when you want to encourage insights, sell-in big ideas or influence attitudes. Other strategies may work at an intellectual level, but are unlikely to provide the emotional engagement needed to bring about lasting change.

Guided discovery requires careful design and facilitation:

- The tasks that learners are set must be carefully designed to draw out key issues that are meaningful to their jobs.

- The tasks should be challenging but must not seem unachievable.

- The learner must be able to relate to the issues raised by a task.

- The learner should not feel they are being manipulated into taking a position that they do not really believe in.

- Ideally the learner should be able to experiment with different approaches without fear of criticism.

- The facilitator (should there be one) should resist the temptation to give advice unless their expertise is called upon by the learner.

In summary

Guided discovery works best when the topic is less black and white, when successful performance depends on making judgements in a wide variety of situations. When poorly designed and facilitated, discovery learning will seem pointless, perhaps even manipulative; well managed, and the result could be much deeper learning. As Carl Rogers once warned us[13], 'Nothing that can be taught is worth learning.'

EXPLORATION

So what is it?

Exploration is by far the most learner-centred of the four strategies and the only one that relies on the learner to make all the choices. It also represents the closing of the circle, because as with exposition, the first strategy we looked at, the learning design is both simple and relatively unstructured, in stark contrast to instruction and guided discovery.

13_ On becoming a person by Carl Rogers, Constable (2004). Rogers also said 'The only person who is educated is the one who has learned how to learn – and change.' Oscar Wilde is also often quoted as saying, 'Nothing that is worth knowing can be taught'.

With the exploration strategy, each learner determines their own learning process, taking advantage of resources provided not only by teachers and trainers but also by peers. What they take out of this process is entirely individual and largely unpredictable. As such, exploration may seem a relatively informal strategy, but no less useful for that. In fact it's probably the way that a great deal of learning takes place.

How about some examples?

Exploration may play a small part in a formal course; perhaps a handout, a job aid or a list of books or links that learners can dip into if they wish. On the other hand, it could just as easily form the basis for a complete just-in-time performance support system in the workplace.

What interaction takes place?

Exploration is an interactive experience. At the very least, the learner must have a high degree of control over what information they access, when and how. Ideally they will also have access to experts and peers with whom they can share perspectives, experiences and resources, and obtain answers to questions.

When should I use it?

Exploration is unlikely to be used as the sole strategy, particularly with an audience of novices or dependent learners. However, it works well as a way for learners to follow up their interest after a formal course. More importantly, it can form the basis for a comprehensive programme to provide job-related information on demand. This can go further than top-down efforts to provide packaged information and support services such as help desks; it can extend to the use of all manner of social media technologies – communities of practice, forums, wikis, blogging and so on – to enable employees to share expertise on a peer-to-peer basis.

Any tips?

The role you play is clearly going to be very different from the three previous strategies. With exploration, the emphasis shifts 'from courses to resources', so what is needed is no longer a lecturer, instructor or a facilitator, but more a *curator*. What's important here is to smooth the way for learners to find the resources they need and to locate like-minded peers. As curator, you may find yourself categorising and organising content and making learners aware of significant new offerings. You also have a role in ensuring the infrastructure is in place to support content sharing, online search, the setting up of communities of practice, finding experts and much more.

In summary

Exploration is not a universal strategy by any means. Novices and dependent learners will struggle with so little structure and direction. Important top-down initiatives cannot rely on such woolly and inconsistent outcomes. But there's no doubt that the trend is towards more learner-centred approaches; more pull less push, more just-in-time than just-in-case, more flexibility and less structure. The key, as ever, is not in following the fashion, but knowing when the time is right to use each of these strategies appropriately.

SO WHAT NOW?

Some learning professionals stick to one of the strategies almost as a matter of faith – it sums up their philosophy of how learning should be achieved. And for some organisations, the strategy that they use for learning is so pervasive that it has almost become a cultural expectation. But in practice, it pays to remain agnostic.

> Each of these strategies has its place, depending on what needs to be learned and by whom. The trick is to use your judgement in determining which strategy to use and when.

Use it or lose it

A good start would be to reflect on the learning solutions for which you are currently responsible. What learning strategies are used within these solutions? Why did you select these strategies? Do you still feel these are the correct choices?

Move on to look at a solution that you are currently considering. Find out as much as you can about the learning requirement and the characteristics of your audience. Ask yourself which strategy or combination of strategies would work best. Check your ideas out against the guidelines presented here.

SUMMARY

	Exposition	*Instruction*	*Guided discovery*	*Exploration*
Nature of the learning experience	Learning content is delivered to the learner.	From the general to the specific / theory to practice; questioning and practical exercises are used to check for learning at each stage.	From the specific to the general; practical exercises and real-world experiences provide a basis for reflection and insight.	The learner uses their own initiative to satisfy their particular needs, making use of available resources.
Role of the learning professional	Subject expert	Instructor / instructional designer	Facilitator	Curator
Outcomes	Communication of the material according to an established curriculum; how much of this is retained will vary widely.	Improvements in knowledge and skills, with relatively predictable results based on specific objectives.	Insights and possible attitudinal shifts, varying from learner to learner.	Learners access whatever expertise it is they need; the outcomes are entirely unpredictable.
Nature of the interaction	Minimal – perhaps some Q&A.	Q&A, practical exercises and assessments.	Structured exercises, discussions.	Ad-hoc, largely peer-to-peer.

	Exposition	*Instruction*	*Guided discovery*	*Exploration*
Suitable for which learners	Anyone, but where this is used as the predominant strategy, particularly independent learners and those with prior knowledge and experience.	Anyone, particularly novices.	Anyone, as long as they are well supported and personal risk is minimised.	Independent learners; those with prior knowledge and experience.
Suitable for which types of learning	Familiarity with a body of knowledge.	Developing new skills and acquiring black-and-white knowledge.	Gaining insights into principles; buying into big ideas; attitude shifting; refining skills.	Just-in-time information; knowledge updates; going beyond the curriculum; creating new knowledge.

BLENDING BY SOCIAL CONTEXT

OVERVIEW

We have all at one time or another learned in a variety of social contexts. You might find this concept a little abstract, but it simply describes who is with us when we learn. Are we learning alone, with one other person, with a group of fellow learners or alongside others in a wider community?

Self-study

Self-study is learning alone. It can range from, at one extreme, reading a book to, at the other, engaging in a complex computer simulation. It might also consist of individual practice, perhaps learning an instrument, rehearsing a presentation or programming a computer. It provides us with a great deal of flexibility as learners because we control the pace at which we learn as well as when, where and for how long. Self-study can stand alone but works best in conjunction with other social contexts. It also relies on a fair amount of self-motivation and discipline.

One-to-one

We can learn one-to-one with an instructor, a coach, a mentor or a subject expert. This process can be conducted on-job, off-job or remotely. One-to-one learning is individualised, which makes it fast and potentially highly effective, but success depends heavily on the quality of the person with whom we are interacting. One-to-one learning makes a valuable contribution but is extremely costly when compared with other approaches. As a result, it is usually rationed to those situations where there is no other option or where the benefits justify the expense.

Group

When we learn with a group, we expand the resources available to us as learners to include our fellow learners. This can provide useful benefits in terms of shared insights and experiences, mutual support and a degree of peer pressure. Group learning can take place live in a physical or virtual classroom. It can also happen at the learner's pace using email, forums and similar tools.

Community

Increasingly we reach out to a wider community to learn, beyond the small groups that we typically encounter in a formal learning setting. These peer groups could take many forms, for example, the employees who work in our company, those who we interact with on a social network, the members of a professional association, the attendees at a conference or even all those three billion people out there who use the Internet. This form of learning could happen in a physical space (such as at a conference) but is perhaps more likely these days to take place online.

How do we interact in these contexts?

Self-study	One-to-one	Group	Community
Learner-content	Learner-teacher	Learner-learner and learner-teacher	Learner-learner

The effectiveness of each of these four contexts will depend to a great extent on the quality of the interaction that is provided, whether that relates to the ability of the learner to control the experience, the availability of personalised feedback, the ability to ask and get answers to questions, or the facility to share perspectives and experiences.

Putting these to use

Each of these social contexts has major advantages, but also some significant drawbacks. The art is to use each social context in those situations in which its benefits can be usefully exploited and its limitations minimised. In practice this often means using them in combination, as ingredients in a blended solution.

SELF-STUDY

So what is it?

Self-study is learning alone, without access to tutors, coaches, subject experts, peers or any other human beings with whom you might like to interact. It might also occur in the presence of other people, with whom the learner *chooses* not to

interact[14]. This doesn't mean that self-study cannot be interactive, just that the interaction is limited to the materials themselves. If those materials are delivered by a computer, then the interactivity can be very rich indeed (think of a computer game or simulation) – it just doesn't involve humans.

14_ My colleague Phil Green recalls an educational technique used some years ago called USSR (uninterrupted sustained silent reading), which involved children and adults all reading material of their own choice in the same place at the same time without interruption, and it had a measurable impact on the motivation of both to develop a reading habit. You could argue that this experience was collaborative, even if there was no direct interaction between the participants.

How about some examples?

A wide variety of methods can be employed in a self-study context, including questionnaires, assignments, assessments, interactive lessons, games, simulations and scenarios. Self-study activities could also involve the learner in reflecting or action planning, as well as reading, watching and listening to learning content.

Self-study is essentially *asynchronous*, in that it does not require the learner to coordinate timing with any other party. It can be accomplished in any physical setting, with or without the aid of packaged materials.

What are the advantages?

One of the key advantages of self-study is that the learner can work at their own pace. Surveys tell us how much learners value this facility. Synchronous (live) learning can be valuable but it is more stressful for the learner, who is compelled to go at the same pace as the group as a whole.

Self-study also allows the learner to undertake their learning in small chunks, which is valuable because it reduces the danger of cognitive overload and allows time for reflection.

Novices are particularly susceptible to overload and will find it hard to concentrate on new material for more than 20 minutes or so.

Thirdly, self-study is useful because it can be accessed on demand. Learning does not have to wait until an activity can be coordinated with a group of other learners that has the same need.

In short, self-study provides learners with much greater control over the learning process and, for many adults, this is inherently motivating. As a result, some learners deliberately choose this approach over alternatives that provide more interaction with teachers and other learners.

Self-study also has economic benefits. Assuming that you have a sufficiently large audience to justify the development of self-study learning materials, you will obtain substantial savings in trainer costs. And interactive, self-study has also been proven to be at least twice as quick as the equivalent classroom training.

And the disadvantages?

We are social animals and it is natural for us to want interaction with other human beings at some stage in our learning. The social component allows us to share our experiences, test out ideas, obtain support and compare perspectives. We may also need to seek clarification, challenge ideas, receive feedback and benchmark our progress against others. For this reason, self-study works best when integrated to some extent with other social contexts.

Having said that, the self-study learner is not usually completely alone. They will often take advantage of colleagues at work or online, as well as friends and family, as sources of support and assistance

---

Most learners would also confess to the difficulty they have in maintaining the self-discipline needed to learn alone.

Somehow there is always some other activity that seems more urgent than our study programme. Hard experience suggests that prolonged periods of self-study need to be timetabled with regular milestones to be reached by specific dates.

Self-study is also limited in the facility it provides for authentic practice, particularly of interpersonal and motor (physical) skills. Sometimes simulators can overcome the limitations, but these are complex and expensive to develop or purchase.

So when should I use it?

Self-study can be used on a stand-alone basis for short interventions such as knowledge updates. It can also form a valuable component in just about any other type of learning intervention, working alongside one-to-one, group and community-based methods.

ONE-TO-ONE

So what is it?

One-to-one learning involves the learner and one other person who is providing the learner with some sort of assistance in the learning process. This person could be labelled an instructor, a coach, a subject expert, a mentor or any number of other things. Learning as a pair with a fellow learner does not constitute one-to-one learning as far as we're concerned – we can regard that as a small group.

One-to-one learning is as old as the human race itself.

From time immemorial, more experienced people have taken on the responsibility for passing on their knowledge and skills to those who are starting off on their learning journey.

How about some examples?

One-to-one learning can employ very different strategies, from simply providing the learner with knowledge (exposition), to a more structured transfer of skills (instruction, perhaps through an apprenticeship), to a coaching relationship (a form of guided discovery), to a more back-seat role in which the learner takes the initiative and the second person acts as a sort of curator (exploration).

We normally think of one-to-one learning as taking place face to face, typically on the job, but there is no reason why it shouldn't be carried out remotely, whether that's live (using the telephone or tools like Skype) or with more flexible timing (using anything from letters to email).

What are the advantages?

The principal advantage of learning one-to-one is that the learner can receive individual attention; there is no guarantee that this will happen, but the potential is there and it would be rare for an instructor or coach not to respond to the progress being made by the learner or to their particular goals. This personalisation explains why one-to-one learning is so effective and why many people choose to learn this way if the opportunity is made available and the cost is affordable.

The relative privacy of a one-to-one relationship also removes some of the fear of embarrassment that can be present in group environments. Unless for some reason the instructor or coach is particularly intimidating, the learner should feel comfortable asking as many questions as they want, without the risk of looking stupid in front of their peers. This could be one of the reasons why so many senior managers ask for individual instruction or coaching!

Another advantage is that one-to-one learning can be carried out in the work environment, which will usually be impractical for a group. Survey after survey tells us that learners favour on-job training, and this is understandable because the whole experience is so much more authentic.

We learn best when the environment in which we practise is as similar as possible to the environment in which we will be applying our new skills.

whether that's driving a car, operating a lathe or answering customer queries.

In terms of flexibility and accessibility, one-to-one learning will typically be easier to organise than group learning, simply because there are fewer people to coordinate. Having said that, self-study and interacting with an online community are always going to be a learner's quickest options.

And the disadvantages?

Many of us will have experienced the negative effects of a poor one-to-one instructor or coach. Normally, the only option is to call a halt to the relationship and find someone else. Clearly the same can happen in a group learning environment such as a classroom, but here the effects can be moderated by the value gained from interactions with your peers.

In a one-to-one situation, the two parties really do have to get on.

Another problem is that the learner has no way to benchmark their performance against their peers, as they would if they were learning in a group. Neither do they get the benefit of differing perspectives and experiences.

From an economic perspective, one-to-one learning is expensive, time-consuming for the instructor or coach, and hard to scale. It simply does not make sense to major on this form of learning unless the need for individualised learning is business critical or when the learner is prepared to pay the full cost, as they might do if they wanted to learn a sport like tennis.

So when should I use it?
It will not always be useful to include a one-to-one component in a blend, but there are many situations where it will be valuable, if only to handle the learner's queries or to provide confidential feedback. Bear in mind that, if it goes on too long, one-to-one learning is tiring for both the instructor/coach and the learner. Better to use it in small doses.

GROUP

So what is it?
When we learn in a group we have the opportunity to share the experience with a number of fellow learners. Typically these will be the people attending the same classroom event or meeting as ourselves or participating in the same online/blended learning cohort. Learning in a group will normally also provide us with the opportunity to interact with a teacher, instructor or facilitator.

It is important to note that group learning provides the *potential* for interaction with peers, but that this does not occur automatically. Learners may sit in the same classroom but interact with no-one, except perhaps a teacher or trainer. This is not what we are referring to as group learning.

How about some examples?
We all have plenty of experience of learning in groups, both at school and probably in our working lives. Typically groups of learners are formed for the purposes of some live event, such as a physical or virtual classroom session, but they could persist over a longer period in the form of a cohort of online/blended learners or an action learning set.

Live groups do allow for more free-flowing conversation, as well as speedier feedback and answers to questions, but they are not the only way for groups to interact. The idea that group members can work together at their own pace is perhaps unique to the online age. Using email, forums, wikis and the like, learners can obtain many of the benefits of working with a live group but with the flexibility to learn when they want.

Many learning activities, such as role-play, discussion or group projects, depend on there being one or more groups of learners. Other activities, such as lectures and presentations, may regularly take place in groups but could just as easily be delivered as packaged materials, such as videos, consumed on an individual basis.

What are the advantages?
The shift over the years from one-to-one to group learning has taken place largely for practical reasons: it is clearly more economical to share the expertise of a teacher, trainer or facilitator with a number of people at the same time. If you were cynical, you could also argue that the main reason children spend all day at school in classrooms is because it frees up their parents to work and carry out other tasks.

However, there are many benefits to learning in groups that are related to the nature of the learning experience. In a group the learner benefits from multiple perspectives, a wealth of varied experience, mutual support, and the ability to benchmark their progress against others. A certain amount of peer pressure also arises, as learners strive to ensure they are not left behind. Taken to extremes, this form of competition can be stressful and get in the way of learning, but in normal circumstances it is likely to spur everybody on.

As we have noted above, some learning activities, such as role-play, discussion and group projects, require interaction between learners. If these are necessary to achievement of the learning objectives, then some element of group work will obviously have to be included.

Lastly, there is an important secondary benefit from learning in a group of strangers – the people that you encounter can become valuable contacts. There is a degree of serendipity to this, of course – you often do not know in advance whether you will have anything valuable in common with the people with which you learn. We are all capable of learning to a degree on our own initiative, hunting down information on the Internet and with our

day-to-day colleagues, but sometimes we simply don't know what we don't know, so we don't go looking. On the other hand, a chance encounter with a fellow learner can open up a wealth of possibilities – maybe a product we'd never heard of, or a method for solving a problem that we had never considered.

And the disadvantages?

When you move from one-to-one to group learning then the needs of the individual learner have to be compromised to some extent to meet the needs of the group. Good teachers, trainers and facilitators can adapt to some extent to meet the needs of individual learners, but there is a limit to what is possible. By and large, the greater the size of the group, the less attention each learner will receive.

While humans are, generally speaking, social animals, not everyone will be comfortable learning in a group.

Some find it frustrating that they cannot control the pace; some resent the fact that, in group activities, some members contribute very little, yet claim their share of the credit; some are afraid that they will be embarrassed in front

of their peers. These difficulties can be tackled, but this requires skilled facilitation.

A simple practical problem is that group learning is harder to organise and so this will not always be the best option when the learner's needs are urgent.

So when should I use it?

The simple answer is not to go for group learning unless there is a real practical benefit to be gained from group activities. There is little point gathering as a group to watch a lecture or a presentation, unless there are going to be sufficient opportunities for meaningful interaction.

Group size also makes a difference. Fay, Garrod and Carletta (2000)[15] found that 'in small, 5-person groups, the communication is like dialogue and members are influenced most by those with whom they interact in the discussion. However, in large, 10-person groups, the communication is like a serial monologue and members are influenced most by the dominant speaker.'

15_ *Group discussion as interactive dialogue or serial monologue: The influence of group size, Fay, Garrod and Carletta, Psychological Science (2000)*

COMMUNITY

So what is it?

Community learning is learning from our peers, beyond the confines of those people participating in a typical small course or working together as a sub-group of a much larger course. We can define 'peers' quite broadly to include those members of any community to which we ourselves belong, for example, our fellow employees at our place of work; those who we link up with on Twitter, Facebook and other social networks; those who belong to the same voluntary associations as us, such as professional bodies, political parties or religious groups; those attending the same face-to-face event as us, such as a conference; those participating with us in a MOOC – a massive open online course, with many thousands of students; the readers of a particular newspaper or those who follow a particular TV programme; or, in the widest sense of all, everyone who uses the Internet.

How about some examples?

The most common ways to learn in a community context are by seeking answers to specific questions (perhaps by using an online forum), by sharing our expertise and experiences (say by posting a video on YouTube) and by co-constructing knowledge (as with the Wikipedia). All of these examples are online, but similar results could be achieved by attending large, face-to-face events such as conferences.

What are the advantages?

Perhaps the key advantage of learning in a wider community context is that your chances of finding people with whom you can profitably interact are increased by sheer weight of numbers.

> However minority your interest, somewhere in those three billion Internet users out there, you will find plenty of people just like you.

This facility will be particularly valuable when what you need to know is not clearly described in existing content (books, web articles, reference manuals, etc.) or when you know it is there somewhere but you simply cannot find it. A quick post to Twitter or some specialist online forum could get you a response in no time at all. And the process is not one-way – you are as likely to help others as they are to help you. On the Internet, everyone is a teacher as well as a learner. No-one knows everything and everyone knows something.

Another way that the wider community can be helpful is in testing out ideas or comparing options. You may have been provided with an expert view through a more formal channel, but you don't feel entirely happy with what you've been told, so you look around to find out what others think. There is a wider trend for people to value the judgements of peers more highly than expert opinion, and we are already seeing that trend mirrored in a learning context.

Another possible benefit stems from the relative anonymity you can achieve when interacting online – particularly if you are not identified by your real name. This can reduce some of the vulnerability some people feel in asking questions of others. In a large enough community, no-one knows or cares whether you're asking stupid questions or expressing off-the-wall opinions.

And the disadvantages?

The potential disadvantages of interacting with strangers are well documented. While you may be relatively safe collaborating with fellow employees on an intranet, out there on the Internet there is a small minority of idiots and people who would do you harm. Most of us are acutely sensitised to the little signs that give away those people whom we should probably avoid, even when we only interact with them using text, but we cannot assume this skill is universal.

We should also be wary of assuming that, because lots of people say the same thing, it is necessarily true. 'Groupthink' occurs when the desire for conformity in a community results in an incorrect or unwise conclusion. Such groups often isolate themselves from contradictory opinion in order to preserve this uniformity. In the words of American comedian George Carlin: 'Never underestimate the power of stupid people in large groups.'

Search engine algorithms can also serve to reinforce our predispositions, by showing us more of the things that we already agree with[16].

Finally, information that is provided informally and which has not been vetted by experts could be unreliable. More often than not, the members of the community will spot inaccuracies and correct them without intervention, but in those cases where the veracity of factual information is critical, it might be necessary for some oversight of the community's interactions.

So when should I use it?
In the context of a formal intervention, interaction with a wider community is most likely to occur in the Follow-up phase, as the learner makes the transition from the confines of a course to continuing developing their skills through their everyday work. However, in a MOOC, interaction with the entire body of students may be routine throughout the programme.

Of course, 'social learning' as it is sometimes described, does not need to have any association with a course, nor does it have to be prescribed by the leaders and managers of a community. In most cases now, people just do it.

16_ If this idea interests you, my colleague Barry Sampson suggests you check out http://dontbubble.us/ and https://medium.com/message/the-algorithm-giveth-but-it-also-taketh-b7efad92bc1f

SUMMARY

	Self-study	One-to-one	Group	Community
Advantages	The learner can study at his or her own pace. The learner can determine when they learn and for how long. The learner is not held back by having to organise their learning to suit others. The learner has the time and space to properly reflect on their learning.	The learner gets individual attention. The learner may feel freer to ask questions and experiment without fear of embarrassment. Learning can take place on the job, which allows for more authentic practice. One-to-one sessions are easier to schedule than group sessions.	The learner benefits from multiple perspectives, mutual support, and the ability to benchmark their progress against others. The learner can engage in learning activities with others. Opportunities can arise for learners to make useful contacts.	In a wider community, there will usually be someone who can help you or who you can help. Large numbers of people working together can create great things, e.g. Wikipedia.

	Self-study	One-to-one	Group	Community
Disadvantages	The learner could feel isolated. Without a strict schedule with deadlines, the learner may lack the necessary self-discipline to engage in learning activities. The learner has no-one to answer their questions. The learner has no-one with whom to share their successes or compare perspectives.	Much depends on the quality of the instructor/coach and the relationship between them and the learner. The learner has no way of benchmarking their progress against others or comparing perspectives. One-to-one learning is expensive and time-consuming for the instructor/coach.	The needs of the individual learner can be compromised to meet the needs of the group. Peer pressure can prove stressful to some learners. Group learning is harder to organise and may not be appropriate when the learner's needs are urgent.	There are hazards when interacting with people you do not know. Information and advice offered by the community may not be reliable or sensible.

A COMPENDIUM OF TEACHING

AND LEARNING METHODS

METHODS ASSOCIATED WITH EXPOSITION

Method	The function this performs	Typical social context(s)
Delivery of information about the curriculum	Provides the learner with an advance organiser.	The learner accesses the information alone.
Delivery of learning content	As you would expect, what this does is provide the learner with access to content. Whether this results in any learning depends on factors such as whether the learner is paying attention, whether the learner finds the material engaging, whether the learner is overloaded, whether the material is clearly organised and presented, and whether the content is optimised for learning (for example, using storytelling and/or visual aids).	The learner accesses the content alone, when this content takes the form of books, videos or audio recordings; or as part of a group, when the content is presented through live lectures and presentations.
Q&A	Where this is available and the learner feels confident to make use of the facility, this provides a useful opportunity to clarify meaning, seek further information or challenge the content.	One-to-one or in a group.
Essay-style examinations	This isn't really exposition, but it is a common accompaniment to courses for which exposition is the dominant approach (academic courses in particular). It requires a lot of human effort to read and mark essays, but we are beginning to see the arrival of intelligent systems that do a credible job.	The learner alone.

METHODS ASSOCIATED WITH INSTRUCTION

Method	The function this performs	Typical social context(s)
Delivery of objectives and other information about the process	This provides the learner with an advance organiser. It also makes clear what knowledge and skills they will be required to demonstrate if the instruction is to be deemed successful.	The learner accesses this alone through some form of interactive self-study, otherwise one-to-one or in a group instruction session.
Assessment of prior knowledge and skill	First of all, this will inform the instructor (or the instructional materials, if these are intelligent enough) so the instruction can be adapted accordingly. Secondly, in a self-study context, and assuming the learner has control over what material they cover, this will allow the learner to make informed choices about their programme of study. Finally, and assuming there is a similarly formatted post-assessment, this makes it possible to measure the progress made as a result of the instruction.	As above

Method	The function this performs	Typical social context(s)
Delivery of learning content	This is how knowledge content is presented to the learner. Whether this contributes to achievement of the learning objectives depends on factors such as whether the learner is paying attention, whether the learner finds the material engaging, whether the learner is overloaded, whether the material is relevant to the learning objectives, whether the material is clearly organised and presented, and whether the content is optimised for learning (for example, using story telling and/or visual aids). If you are teaching a task, rather than just providing knowledge, it is important to concentrate on the essential information that the learner will need. A good rule of thumb would be 'to provide just enough information to allow the learner to start practising and no more'.	As above
Use of questions to check and reinforce learning content	One of the advantages of instruction over exposition is the frequent use of interactivity to attract and retain the learner's attention, check comprehension, encourage the learner to explore the content in meaningful ways, and put the content into context. Regular, meaningful interactivity may be more demanding for both the instructor and the learner, but it will improve your chances of success.	As above

Method	The function this performs	Typical social context(s)
Tests of knowledge	A well-designed test, that is closely aligned to the knowledge objectives, will provide an indication of what the learner knows at the point of time at which the test was taken. However, knowledge fades quickly and more reliable results will be achieved by testing some time after the learning was first accomplished, perhaps even at intervals over days, weeks and months.	As above
Delivery of worked examples and demonstrations of skilled performance	When the aim is to teach a task (rather than just knowledge), an essential step on the journey is to demonstrate the task, ideally in a variety of different contexts, starting with the most straightforward and graduating to more complex or unusual situations.	As above
Examples of how not to do something	There has been controversy about the validity of 'negative modelling' since the first Video Arts training films made us laugh by showing us just how badly things can be done. The detractors believe it reinforces what not to do. The believers would explain that we have always learned by watching people make mistakes and that these situations are extremely memorable. Clearly negative modelling should be combined with showing the positive.	As above

Method	The function this performs	Typical social context(s)
Role-play and other forms of simulated practice	The only way for a learner to acquire skills is to practise. Ideally, the first opportunities to practise should be as safe as possible, for the learner (no risk of injury, whether physically or psychologically), for the organisation (no risk of physical damage to equipment or to reputation) and to third parties such as customers. Role-play is a safe way to practise social skills (although more popular with instructors than with learners). The equivalent for motor skills would be a simulator.	As above
Repetitive drilling	The more a skill is practised, the easier it becomes. Drills provide an intensive burst of practice. Examples include typing exercises, solving mathematical problems, and repeating a physical action such as catching a ball. Drills could also be used to rehearse important knowledge such as vocabulary, times tables, anatomical terms or historical facts.	As above
Receiving feedback on performance	Practice is not enough if all you are doing is reinforcing bad habits. Although a learner may be able to critique their performance to some degree by comparing what they have done against a model or by reviewing against a checklist, it will usually be helpful if more objective feedback is provided, whether that comes from an instructor, from peers or from software, or from the results achieved by the learner.	As above

Method	The function this performs	Typical social context(s)
Supervised on-job practice	Safe practice, using methods such as role-play and simulation, makes a useful contribution to the Skills Journey but at some point the learner has to put their skills into practice in a more authentic situation. Supervised on-job practice, with an instructor, coach, or supervisor, maintains some scaffolding for the learner as they progress through the early stages of 'conscious competence'.	One-to-one

METHODS ASSOCIATED WITH GUIDED DISCOVERY

Method	The function this performs	Typical social context(s)
Surveys and questionnaires	One way for the learner to achieve insights is to reflect on their own preferences and behaviour, or on the observations that others have made about them. This process might be repeated before and after an intervention to measure what has changed.	The learner completes these alone or, when in the form of a 360-degree survey, with a group or wider community.
Clarifying goals	While, in an instructional strategy, the process is driven from the top-down by learning objectives, with guided discovery the learner's own goals become much more of an influence. Depending on the situation, the learner alone may decide on what their goals should be, but there will often be others with a keen interest in a learner's performance, not least managers and coaches.	The learner does this alone or with a manager or coach.
Breaking the ice	Because guided discovery is so often stimulated by social interaction, it is important that learners quickly become comfortable in each other's company, physically or virtually. Ice-breakers are activities not directly related to the topic in hand, but which encourage learners to open up to and trust each other.	With a group

Method	The function this performs	Typical social context(s)
Sharing personal information, including goals	When guided discovery is taking place in the context of a group, it is important that the learner is able to share their goals with facilitators and fellow learners. In that way, all parties can be more supportive in helping the learner to achieve their desired outcomes.	With a group
Activities that turn learners in to teachers	In an expositional or instructional context, the subject expert and/or instructor provide whatever information learners will need; where the strategy is one of guided discovery, this is an opportunity missed. Activities in which learners, alone or in groups, are assigned to hunt down information and then present this back to the whole cohort, provide all sorts of opportunities for insights. There are also benefits in terms of the acquisition of knowledge, because for many the best way to learn something is to be required to teach it. To put something across clearly, you really do have to understand it well.	The learner alone or as part of a group.

Method	The function this performs	Typical social context(s)
Case studies and scenarios	Case studies and scenarios provide a way for learners to act as problem-solvers in the situations encountered by others, whether real or imagined. They provide concrete examples of abstract ideas, practice in problem-solving, and the opportunity for all sorts of insights into cause and effect relationships. Case studies and scenarios are memorable because, at heart, they are stories, and these will always be more memorable than models and other abstractions. And assuming they are well matched to the audience's abilities, they can be extremely challenging and engaging. Having trouble getting your senior managers and professionals interested in a subject? Just provide them with a tricky case study that provides an opportunity for them to test their skills and impress their peers.	The learner alone or as part of a group.

Method	The function this performs	Typical social context(s)
Practical assignments	Practical assignments provide a chance for learners to put their thinking into practice and to test this against reality. Individual assignments provide a better indicator of how far the individual learner has progressed, but restrict the number of perspectives to which the learner will be exposed. Group assignments can be tricky to organise and there is no doubt that some learners find them frustrating. To some extent this is because the group rather than the individual learner controls the pace, but problems can also arise when some group members contribute less than others. On the other hand, group assignments provide plenty of opportunity for learners to share thoughts and expertise, and to experience teamwork. To maximise participation, restrict group size to four people or less.	The learner alone or as part of a group.

Method	The function this performs	Typical social context(s)
Simulations	In the context of an instructional strategy, a simulation provides an opportunity to rehearse skills, but it can function even more effectively as a tool for guided discovery. Imagine a simulation that allowed you to experiment with different economic, political, social or commercial strategies. You'll find these already exist, if only as video games. Branching scenarios, a form of e-learning, are also essentially simulations: you are presented with a series of decisions to make; the choices you make determine how the situation evolves; the outcome of the scenario could be good, bad or neutral; if you are unhappy with how the situation turned out or just like to play, you can retrace your steps and try a different approach. Scenarios are popular – you can see why.	The learner alone or as part of a group.
Debriefing sessions	In a self-study context, it will be up to the learner to come to their own insights by reflecting on the activities to which they have been exposed. In a more sophisticated scenario or simulation, the software may give the learner a helping hand. In a group context, time can be set aside to ensure that reflection takes place. The primary role of the facilitator will be to ask the questions, not to provide answers, although they may be able to reinforce or challenge the thinking of the group by reference to models, research and experience.	One-to-one or group

Method	The function this performs	Typical social context(s)
Coaching sessions	Coaching brings together many aspects of guided discovery. The coach helps the learner to clarify their goals and establish plans; at the next session they then debrief what has occurred and start the process again. Coaches help learners to continuously develop their skills but also to gain insights into the big ideas that can determine success or failure.	One-to-one
Action learning sets	An action learning set provides another example of the many ways in which guided discovery can be facilitated. The set is typically made up of managers or other professionals with real-life problems to solve. The meetings of the set allow participants to describe the goals they are looking to accomplish, their ideas for ways of meeting these goals, their progress to that point and their learning as a result of their experiences. The group context allows participants to offer support and encouragement and for further insights to occur through the experiences of others.	Group

Method	The function this performs	Typical social context(s)
Discussions	Discussions occur in all sorts of learning contexts, but particularly guided discovery. They can be used to agree goals, debate alternative approaches or interpretations, compare experiences, extract meaning from these experiences and much more. There is some evidence to suggest that really free-flowing discussions work best with groups of four or less. When groups get bigger than this, rather than dialogue, you experience a sort of 'serial monologue[19]', as participants carefully prepare their next contribution rather than helping to bring about a conclusion.	Group
Learners maintain a learning journal	The concept of a learning journal is not new, but historically this was something private, like a diary. Blogging has rather changed this, as the writer becomes a 'learning journalist', sharing their reflections with others. Different formats will work in different situations: perhaps only the learner sees their journal entries, or just the learner and the facilitator; alternatively, everyone in the group could see the postings, perhaps even everyone on the Internet. The purpose of the journal is to provide a formal place in the structure of an intervention for personal reflection. Sometimes the act of articulating what they have experienced will be all that learners need to clarify their insights so they can be tested through interaction with others and through real-life application.	The learner does this alone but can share their postings with a teacher and/or a group and/or a wider community.

METHODS ASSOCIATED WITH EXPLORATION

Method	The function this performs	Typical social context(s)
Accessing suggested books, videos, websites, etc.	You'll notice that all of these methods are expressed from the learner's perspective, which is because, with the exploration strategy, the learner controls what happens. However, from your perspective as a designer of blended solutions, there is still work to do, helping the learner to find the information they will find most useful. We call this content curation[20]. The curator of an exhibition in a museum assembles exhibits from the museum's collection that they believe will provide a satisfying experience for a particular target audience. Similarly, the content curator narrows down the search for the learner, picking out books, videos and websites that should probably be explored first. Of course, the learner can choose to ignore all this and go their own way. Content curation is particularly valuable for novices who don't know how to pick out the most useful items from a Google search. Of course, Google's algorithms do their best to perform a job of curation, but sometimes humans know best, at least for now!	The learner alone

19_ See Group Discussion as Interactive Dialogue or as Serial Monologue: The Influence of Group Size by Nicolas Fay, Simon Garrod and Jean Carletta, Psychological Science (2000).

20_ I was introduced to the important role of content curation by Julie Wedgwood, www.juliewedgwood.co.uk.

Method	The function this performs	Typical social context(s)
Accessing reference information and other job aids	Reference information and other job aids, such as decision trees and troubleshooting guides, are essential elements in the Follow-up phase. Much of the information that an employee needs to do their job can be safely referenced as and when needed rather than memorised. Producing this material is an important aspect of the development of a blended solution. Increasingly this will mean online content, accessible on mobile devices.	The learner alone
Establishing communities of interest/practice	Explicit knowledge (the stuff which is easily articulated) can be taught formally or included in reference materials. Tacit knowledge, which describes how problems are solved and decisions made in practice, is better communicated informally. Communities formed around a particular interest or passion provide a means for tacit knowledge to be explored and shared. Online tools mean these communities can easily extend beyond the immediate workplace.	Wider community
Co-constructing content	Another way that knowledge can be shared is through content generated by learners themselves. The most obvious manifestation of this practice is the wiki. Wikipedia provides a startling example of what can be achieved when people collaborate around a task. We take it for granted now, but not so long ago it was just an empty database and many expected it would stay that way.	As a group or wider community

Method	The function this performs	Typical social context(s)
Sharing experiences, ideas and solutions	This is just a catch-all to cover all those situations in which learners collaborate other than through a formal community or a wiki.	As a group or wider community
Receiving mentoring	Mentoring is a one-to-one relationship between someone who has extensive experience and someone who is a relative novice. The role of the mentor is to aid the mentee's development by passing on the benefit of their experience. Normally the mentor is senior to the mentee, but we are beginning to see an increased use of reverse mentoring. Here the more junior person passes on their knowledge of modern approaches (a good example being the use of new technologies) to an older person such as a senior manager.	One-to-one
Having a buddy	Buddying is similar in nature to mentoring, except the buddy is likely to be at a similar level to the learner, but with more experience.	One-to-one
Conducting research	Research is an obvious example of how an exploratory strategy can deliver learning. It is not surprising that the highest levels of educational achievement are focused on this approach. Researchers can go beyond the accumulation of existing thinking – they can push forward the frontiers of knowledge.	The learner alone

Method	The function this performs	Typical social context(s)
Visits	Visits take the learner out of their normal environment to discover what goes on elsewhere – most typically in other parts of their own organisation. These events provide insights into how the work of one part of an organisation affects another. A visit may also be undertaken as a form of benchmarking. The learner visits those who carry out similar functions to themselves in other organisations or different parts of the same organisation (such as other territories).	The learner alone or in groups

Method	The function this performs	Typical social context(s)
Maintaining a portfolio of evidence	A portfolio provides a means for a learner to demonstrate the results of their endeavours, not so much in terms of what they now know but what they can now do. A portfolio demonstrates where a learner has got to, not where they came from – it is output rather than input oriented. As such, it does not require the learner to have undertaken any formal courses, which is why it sits most happily within the exploration strategy.	The learner alone
Being assessed for competence	There is no point assembling a portfolio if no-one sees it. Whether the learner has or has not achieved competence is usually determined by an assessor or the person's manager, but it is also possible for this to be accomplished through peer review.	One-to-one or group

THE

BL

COLLECTION:

PLAN

MANAGEMENT SKILLS GO ACCORDING TO PLAN

This case study demonstrates how an international NGO has been able to provide their managers with the skills they need to operate in the farthest corners of the globe. This feat would not have been possible without the flexibility provided by a carefully crafted blended solution.

TALKING ABOUT THE PLAN CERTIFICATE IN MANAGEMENT

Pam Innes, Director, HR and Organisational Development

Plan is a major global NGO focused on helping children and communities in over 50 countries from the point of view of both long-term development and humanitarian interventions.

I believe that management skills are critical for an organisation such as Plan. Many organisations talk about staff being their greatest asset, but I would argue that, for Plan, they really are.

We need to have hugely well-developed technical skills for our staff to be able to do what they do for the children and communities that we serve. It's also critical to have strong management skills in an organisation where a large number of the staff are going to be in remote locations working quite autonomously.

I believe that management skills are critical for an organisation such as Plan. Many organisations talk about staff being their greatest asset, but I would argue that, for Plan, they really are.

Karen Coleman, Head of Learning

We want our staff to have the underpinning knowledge around management practice, but what's key to this programme is the development of skills and how they translate these back to the workplace and practise them continuously.

The programme is aimed at middle managers and above who have people responsibility, across our 50 countries. Some of these managers would have had elements of management training before, but what the Plan Certificate does is provide the key skills that we think *all* managers should have. By going through the programme, we know that they've got all of the skills we require to deliver our business strategy.

We are a global organisation with a vast number of different cultures. And English isn't always the first language for many of our managers, so that can be challenging. The other constraint that we faced when we first started the programme, although it's getting better, was Internet bandwidth. While people did have access to the Internet, bandwidth wasn't always good and sometimes got in the way for people in remote places.

Julie Ellison, Learning and Development Manager

An applicant to the programme will sign a learning agreement, outlining their commitment to the programme. We also require the manager to agree to the support they're going to provide in the form of coaching.

The application then goes to the Regional Director who will have to prioritise, because we've got more applications than we've got places.

Once an individual has enrolled in the programme, they complete a 360-degree report that includes feedback from their manager, their direct reports and their peer group. This helps them to identify their objectives for the programme.

The first unit introduces participants to the programme, to the methodology and to the technology they'll be using. They also attend a welcome webinar during which they'll have the chance to ask questions, introduce themselves to other participants and start working together.

Overall the programme consists of six units and uses a wide range of learning methodologies. There is self-directed learning, including e-learning modules, TED Talks and surveys to complete. There are also group activities, including forum discussions and assignments, in which learners work in small groups and provide each other with feedback and coaching. There

are also webinars and tutor-marked assignments.

For every unit, the individual sets their learning objectives. During the unit they collect evidence of their use of the various skills and behaviours and at the end of the unit they review their success and plan for future development.

The four-day workshop is the final element. It enables participants to practise and demonstrate the behaviours and skills they've learned throughout the programme.

Before the workshop, they complete their second 360-degree review, which they use to help to identify the skills they want to practise and get coached on during the workshop. They also use this with their manager to identify their learning plan for the future.

Karen
Because participants do a 360-degree analysis both at the beginning and the end of the programme, we're able to demonstrate an uplift in skills to the business each year.

And although the programme was introduced in 2006, we still have a huge demand for places. In fact, two or three years ago, senior management made it mandatory that anyone who wants to be a director in the future must attend the course.

And in 2008, we received external recognition when we won a UK National Training Award.

WHAT PARTICIPANTS HAVE TO SAY

Farrah Naz, Pakistan

An excellent course. There is a combination of various methodologies – we are using online modules, we are interacting with people, we have moderators who can have webinars with us. It's provided an opportunity for interaction as well as self-learning.

Shashike Gamage, Asia Regional Office

The best thing I liked was the blended learning approach. We got a lot of information from the online resources and from webinars, and we also got the opportunity to interact with different colleagues from across the global organisation, which is fantastic. It was also really great to join the workshop and practise some of those skills.

ANALYSED: THE PLAN CERTIFICATE IN MANAGEMENT

The situation	The blend
The need	Plan requires their managers around the world to demonstrate a consistently high level of management skills if they are to deliver on their strategic objectives.
The learning	While Plan wants its managers to be familiar with current thinking about management, the main requirement has been to develop core skills that can be applied and practised continuously.
The learners	The programme is aimed at managers with people responsibility across their 50 countries.
The logistics	English is, in many cases, a second language for participants.
	Internet bandwidth can be a problem in remote locations.

	Methods	*Media*
Preparation	Applicants and their managers sign an agreement to demonstrate their commitment to the programme.	Submitted online
	Participants complete a 360-degree questionnaire to identify priority objectives.	Completed online
	Participants complete an initial module, which introduces them to the programme and to the technology they will be using.	Completed online using Plan's Moodle VLE
	Participants attend an introductory session.	Online using Blackboard Collaborate
Input	Each unit of the course includes self-directed elements, including e-learning modules, videos to watch and reflective assignments.	Accessed online through the VLE
	Many of the units include live sessions run by subject experts.	Online using Blackboard Collaborate
	Group assignments allow participants to work together, share perspectives and provide each other with support.	Groups collaborate in whichever way they see fit, but typically online

	Methods	*Media*
Application	At the end of each unit, participants review the progress they have made towards their objectives with their managers.	Completed locally
	After the final unit, participants complete a second 360-degree survey to identify priorities to be addressed at the workshop.	Completed online
	The four-day workshop provides opportunities for practising skills and celebrating success.	Face to face
Follow-up	Participants agree a learning plan for the future with their managers.	Completed locally

PART 6
MEDIA

LEARNING MEDIA AND THE
EXPLOSION
OF OPPORTUNITY

Very few learning methods are tied to a specific learning medium – they can usually be implemented in more than one way, perhaps online, face to face, even over the phone. It is an important aspect of the *more than* approach that you leave the choice of medium until last:

* *First* you establish the methods that you believe will be effective in meeting the demands of your particular situation.

* *Then* you select the most appropriate media for delivering these methods, looking to optimise flexibility and efficiency without compromising on effectiveness.

The result of this may be a rich blend of different media; on the other hand, it may be that you choose to use the same medium throughout. This is not of any importance – your goal here is to optimise efficiency, not to introduce variety.

MEDIA OPTIONS ARE INCREASING EXPONENTIALLY

For many thousands of years the only practical way for one human being to learn from another was to be present in the same physical space at the same point in time.

Over the years, humans developed the capability to read and write, which provided the potential for some learning to take place in the learner's own time, although the scalability of this approach was heavily constrained until the advent of the printing press.

Books provided the counterbalance to face-to-face learning, by allowing learners more independence and the ability to control the pace at which they learned. Then, the invention of the telephone provided additional connectivity for learners and tutors working at a distance. In the mid-twentieth century, we saw a proliferation of new technologies that allowed for audio and video material to be distributed on recordable media such as tapes and discs, or broadcast to TVs and radios. In the classroom, it became possible to project still images as overhead transparencies and 35mm slides. These media provided teachers and trainers with many new options for enriching the classroom experience or providing learners with new forms of self-study materials.

Until about 1980, most learning professionals would have been able to keep up with all these media options. They would have known when to use each of these media and how. But with the advent of the personal computer and then, ten years later, the Internet, the rate of change really speeded up. As a result, and in many cases with insufficient attention placed on continuous professional development, many teachers and trainers have become overwhelmed by the proliferation of new technologies and the opportunities that these provide.

METHODS DETERMINE EFFECTIVENESS, NOT MEDIA

Let's just pause for a moment to make absolutely clear how methods and media impact on the likely success of your solution.

Broadly speaking, *methods determine effectiveness* – if you choose the right methods and you deliver them well, you are likely to achieve your learning objectives.

A great deal of effort has been put into research to test whether the communications media used for learning have a similar impact on effectiveness. Thomas L. Russell undertook an analysis of more than 350 studies conducted over the past 50 or so years, each attempting to compare the effectiveness of one learning medium with another. The title of Russell's book is *The No Significant Difference Phenomenon*, which says it all.

A meta-analysis of 96 studies, by Sitzmann and others, published in 2006, also makes clear that it's the method, not the delivery medium that makes the difference. When web-based and classroom instruction employing similar methods were compared, there was little or no difference in outcome. That is not to say that the choice of medium is unimportant; it has a big impact on the efficiency and flexibility of the solution, but not so much on its effectiveness.

Needless to say, real-life is not quite this simple. You clearly cannot use *any* medium to deliver *any* method – the medium must have the necessary functionality. So, a book is not a suitable medium with which to hold a discussion (although the book might stimulate a discussion) and you are not going to get very far practising footballing skills on a mobile device (although the device may be useful in modelling those skills). Evidently some common sense is required.

TWO WAYS TO ANALYSE LEARNING MEDIA

There are now so many learning media that it is easy to be overwhelmed by choice. As we discovered with learning methods, it can help to look at the broad categories of media before narrowing down to particular options. Over the following chapters, we will be analysing media in two ways:

1. According to the delivery channel (face to face, offline media, online media)

2. According to the communication mode (same-time or own-time)

We follow this by presenting a compendium of different learning media and by suggesting that we might like to consider a new default option, not face-to-face learning but online and own-time.

BLENDING BY

DELIVERY CHANNEL

OVERVIEW

Learning media provide the means for us to deliver our chosen methods.

Unlike teaching and learning methods, which stay constant over time, media are constantly evolving with new advances in technology.

Face-to-face learning

It might seem odd to think of face-to-face communication as a medium because it depends on no intermediary technology, but it is clearly a means for delivery; in fact for early humans it was the only option available. In an era increasingly dominated by the Internet, face-to-face teaching and training remains the number one choice, whether on-the-job or in a classroom, although it is slowly but surely losing its 'market share'. While face-to-face teaching and training has a number of unique qualities and will always have a place, it cannot deliver the flexibility and scalability of other options.

Within the face-to-face category, we should also include projects, assignments and other practical tasks that learners can complete in whichever way they see fit.

Offline media

When new media gradually became available to provide an alternative to face-to-face learning, starting with the printed book and extending, in the twentieth century, to include all sorts of recordable media, the idea that these were to be consumed 'offline' made no sense. However, now that most new learning media operate in an online context, i.e. through a computer network, it is a useful distinction. Offline media may be in decline as Internet bandwidth becomes ubiquitous, but still provide a useful vehicle for self-study, for those situations in which Internet access is not available.

Online media

Online media require the learner to have access to the Internet (or an organisation's intranet). This may seem like an important barrier but, as connectivity rapidly expands in speed and coverage across the world, this facility will soon be taken for granted just about everywhere. While there are limitations to what can be achieved online, the potential is there to replace a large proportion of the learning that has traditionally been conducted face to face and using offline media with a far more flexible and scalable alternative.

Putting these to use

For each element of your blended solution, your first priority is to select strategies and social contexts that will be effective in delivering on your learning objectives. Then the focus shifts to finding the most flexible and efficient ways of delivering these methods, without compromising on potential effectiveness. And this is where learning media come into play.

LEARNING FACE TO FACE

So what is it?

Face-to-face learning involves two or more participants. It takes place in real-time and with all participants present in the same physical space. This category also provides a home for projects and assignments that are undertaken in whichever way the learner sees fit.

How about some examples?

When we think of face-to-face teaching and training, our thoughts probably jump to the classroom, but all sorts of physical environments can be fruitful in certain situations. Historically, far more face-to-face learning has been conducted on the job than has ever taken place in a classroom, but you'll also see learning taking place in purpose-built workshop environments, where learners can access specialist equipment, as well as on test tracks and playing fields, on mountains and in the water. It all depends on the learning requirement.

What are the advantages?

Face-to-face learning is multi-sensory, in that hearing, sight, smell, taste and touch can all be employed.

While the most important senses for learning are sight and hearing, and computers can accommodate both of these well, there are circumstances in which the other senses can be critical; for example, taste when learning cookery, smell in chemistry, and touch when practising combat skills.

Importantly, in a face-to-face environment, teachers and learners can observe each other's body language in real-time, quickly and easily.

While webcams provide some clues in this regard, the resolution and frame-rate of the image is often poor, and screen real estate does not permit more than a few webcam feeds to be viewed simultaneously. Online video will inevitably improve over time, but for now this is a real issue for any learning in which body language is critical, including much interpersonal skills training and also when there are negative attitudes to be addressed.

Another situation in which a face-to-face context is valuable is when learners need to practise skills in a highly realistic setting. For some occupations, a realistic setting *is* being online, but for most of us realistic means being on the job, with the equipment, people and other physical resources that would be around you every day.

There are other advantages which are less easy to pin down through simple logic but which have an emotional impact. There is something special about being in the same space as others who are experiencing an important event together. While we may be happy to listen to most music on our iPods, watch most sport on TV, and experience drama through film rather than in the theatre, those occasions on which we do take the trouble to be present at a live event are much more memorable – they may even be peak life experiences. Undoubtedly some learning activities – hopefully some of yours – will fall in this category.

Finally, there is an element of serendipitous learning in face-to-face events. It is no coincidence that those with similar technical or professional skills tend to cluster in the same physical locations, as software engineers do in Silicon Valley. These people could all communicate with each other online, but they like to increase their chances for making potentially valuable contacts by using the same stores, cafes and restaurants. And no-one goes to as many conferences as geeks, not necessarily for the presentations (these can be seen anytime on YouTube) but for the networking.

And the disadvantages?

The major problem with learning face to face is that participants have to be present in the same physical location. If everyone works in the same building or on the same site and you have a suitable space in which everyone can meet, then this is not an issue. However, more often than not people will have to travel and sometimes that also means staying overnight. Travel consumes time and money, and it impacts negatively on the environment.

The need to bring people together in a central location has another effect. Even though we know that learning is better accomplished in small chunks[17], face-to-face learning events tend to be measured in days rather than hours. It is simply impractical to have learners travel repeatedly to attend short sessions, even though these may be more effective, so we aggregate large numbers of learning activities into lengthy sessions lasting days.

A side effect of long face-to-face events is that it provides the learner with inadequate opportunities for reflection and personal study.

While real-time interaction with other learners is valuable, you can have too much of a good thing. As ever in blended solutions, balance is everything.

So when should I use it?
Face-to-face learning is too often the default. While it can be powerful, it can also be expensive, time-consuming and inflexible.

Unless all your learners are on the same site, a better strategy might be to regard face-to-face learning as a special case,

17_ See Richard E Mayer's work on cognitive load theory

to be employed when only this will do the job and rarely as the only element in a blend.

OFFLINE MEDIA

So what are they?
In the beginning there was face-to-face learning and it was good. However, over time people realised that it would be valuable to capture knowledge and expertise so it did not have to be passed down by word of mouth and people could learn on their own when there was no teacher to hand. And so people created writing and, after a few more thousands of years, printing; and learning began to accelerate in a way that people had never before experienced.

The printed book is perhaps the most significant example of an offline medium. The term 'offline' encompasses all those technologies that allow people to consume and interact with content asynchronously (in their own time) but which do not require them to be connected to the Internet or some other network such as an intranet. Offline media provided the ideal counterpoint to face-to-face learning until, of course, the Internet came along.

How about some more examples?
Just about all of the technologies that were invented in the twentieth century as means to play back recorded audio and video have been used extensively for self-study, including various forms of tape and disc. Perhaps the most significant of these in the analogue era were the vinyl disc, the audio cassette, VHS tapes and, in the 1980s, videodiscs, which were capable of holding 36 minutes of video and audio on each side or 72,000 still images.

As the move began to digital media, videodiscs were superseded by CD-ROMs, tapes and cassettes by audio CDs, and videocassettes by DVDs. As a medium for self-study, the most popular of these has undoubtedly been the CD-ROM, a form of removable data storage for PCs, capable of holding both multimedia materials and software applications. Until the advent of the Internet, the CD-ROM was the prime carrier for interactive e-learning programmes, and is still useful for that purpose in those locations in which Internet access is unreliable.

The latest development in offline media has been the downloading of digital content (which does, admittedly, require the learner to be online) so that this content can then be accessed offline. The most common examples of this phenomenon are the downloading of audio and video files for playback on iPods, mobile phones and tablets, and e-books for use on devices such as the Kindle, although every time you download a PDF or a PowerPoint to review at your leisure or print out you are essentially doing the same thing. Another example is the use of apps on smartphones or tablets – while some of these require the user to be online, many work completely independently, using code and data that are resident on the device.

What are the advantages?

The principal advantage of an offline medium is that it is not online – it doesn't require the learner to have an adequate Internet connection.

What is 'adequate' will depend on the multimedia elements that comprise your content – text, for example, requires very little bandwidth, whereas video requires a great deal.

Offline media are particularly advantageous when learners need access to top quality media, such as HD video or uncompressed audio. While those with the best Internet connections may be able to stream even the highest quality media online, many will struggle. However, you have to ask yourself how often such high media quality is really important to learning – typically you can make do with formats that are much less demanding in terms of bandwidth.

Some people prefer traditional offline media, such as books and discs, because they like their tactile qualities and enjoy building them into collections. Equally, many younger people might take the opposite position and regard all this stuff as just so much 'clutter'.

And the disadvantages?

The nature of offline media is that every learner has their own copy of the content stored on their PC or mobile device, on disc or in print. This is fine until you need to make a change, because this requires every one of these copies being replaced. By comparison, when working online, there is theoretically only ever one copy of each piece of content, so when this is updated every learner will automatically have access to the latest version.

There is also a time lag inherent in using offline media because they have to be physically shipped or, at very least, downloaded. While this is acceptable in many circumstances, people are becoming increasingly used to the idea of information on demand.

Physical offline media, such as printed books and DVDs, are slow and expensive to produce and deliver. Again this contrasts with online media, for which each new access is almost free (I say 'almost' because online content does have to be hosted on computers and transmitted over networks, all of which have to be paid for – however these costs are dramatically lower than for the physical equivalent).

Finally, there is a limit to how much space any learner can make available on their shelves or on their computer's hard drives for libraries of offline media.

A learner who sets themselves down to study at a PC in the world's largest library will still be less well resourced than another learner with a smartphone and an Internet connection.

So when should I use them?

The most obvious situation in which to use offline media is when you want to make self-study content available but the learner will not have access to a reliable Internet connection when they choose to consume the content. More often than not, in these circumstances you will now choose to make the content available for online download when the learner *does* have access to adequate bandwidth for them to subsequently access. An obvious example would be air or rail travellers who could download content at home or in the office for viewing when they are commuting or on business trips.

Other forms of offline media, such as printed books, CD-ROMs and DVDs are in terminal decline as other, more flexible media become available. However fondly some of us may treasure our collections of these media, the reality is that they are unlikely to feature in your blends beyond the short term.

ONLINE MEDIA

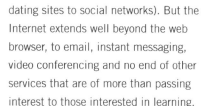

So what are they?

When Sir Tim Berners-Lee launched the World Wide Web back in the early 1990s, the Internet was already well established, with hundreds of thousands of computers connected 24/7 to enable messaging and file sharing across the globe. However, few outside the world of science and technology would have been aware of its existence. The web changed all that, because it provided a standardised and non-proprietary mechanism for publishing textual content on the Internet across all sorts of computing devices, free of charge. While the original target may have been scientists sharing papers, it soon became obvious that anything could be published by anyone to everyone. And that's exactly what happened.

As the Internet became more and more popular and bandwidth improved, the web became more sophisticated, supporting more media types (graphics, then audio and video), more ways to interact with content (like buying a book, registering for an e-newsletter or searching for content) and more ways to communicate with other web users (from chat rooms to forums, blogs to wikis, dating sites to social networks). But the Internet extends well beyond the web browser, to email, instant messaging, video conferencing and no end of other services that are of more than passing interest to those interested in learning.

What all online media have in common is that they are only accessible with an Internet (or perhaps just an intranet) connection. What this definition doesn't convey, however, is the broad scope and amazingly diverse application of this capability.

How about some examples?

Some online media are essentially forms of content, from simple web pages, to elaborate 3D environments, simulations, e-learning modules and videos. What makes these truly online in nature is that none of this content has to be downloaded first and stored on your local device – it is accessed as and when needed over the Internet. The Internet can be used to download content, such as podcasts, films and music, but this content is subsequently accessed offline.

Real online content sits in the cloud waiting for you to access it, as and when needed.

Other online media provide the ability for Internet users to interact with each other in their own time (asynchronously). The obvious example is email, but many other means have evolved including forums, blogs, wikis and social networks. Leaving email to one side, this choice of means for interaction is largely unprecedented in human history. Before the Internet, it was much less practical for distributed groups of people to collaborate in their own time (so not face to face) to discuss, share or co-construct. The impact of this new way of working has been remarkable, with Wikipedia and Facebook as just two examples. Needless to say, the possibilities for learning are enormous.

The third variety of online media includes all those applications that enable same-time (synchronous) communication, such as instant messaging (including tools like Skype), web conferencing (which supports virtual classrooms, webinars and online meetings) and virtual worlds. These tools provide a direct equivalent to face-to-face communication as well as an alternative to the telephone.

What are the advantages?

The primary advantage of online media is that they free the learner from the constraints of space.

Through the Internet, the learner can interact with more than three billion people and trillions of items of content and these numbers can keep rising because there are negligible constraints on expansion. The world's biggest stadium can hold only a tiny fraction of all these Internet users, and the world's greatest library contains nothing like as much content. Given that much of this interpersonal contact and access to content is free, it is no exaggeration to say that the Internet completely changes the game. If you are in doubt, just consider how frequently you use PCs and mobile devices to find information and communicate with friends, family and colleagues. We are different people now, with higher expectations for access to information and participation. We will be baffled if these expectations are not met when we are at work.

Given that online media operate over a network and that every user has access to the same data, it becomes much quicker and easier to deploy content. In the heyday of offline media, books or CDs would have to be manufactured and then distributed physically. Every time there was a modification to the content, the process would have to be repeated. When content is deployed online it can be accessible in minutes, with every user guaranteed to be using the latest version. What's more, there is no penalty for making changes, which means content can be continuously refined to reflect changing circumstances and user feedback.

As we have already seen, the Internet is extremely versatile. It can provide a workable alternative to face-to-face learning and a much more practical way of distributing content than offline media. It goes further than both of its competitors in also allowing large groups of learners to collaborate in their own time. It is possible, in the right circumstances, to deliver a whole blend online without compromise. This may be the exception rather than the rule, but it will be common enough.

And the disadvantages?

The most important disadvantage to all online media is the necessity for the user to have an active Internet connection and, when there is a need to communicate with audio and video, the connection must be a good one. In many parts of the world and in many working contexts, this is not a problem, but high bandwidth is not yet ubiquitous. It will be and sooner than we think.

And, while the online experience approximates what can be achieved face to face or with offline media, it still requires some compromises. Being in the same physical space as other learners still has the potential to be more engaging and memorable. And, for many Internet users without access to extremely good bandwidth, offline media are still capable of a higher quality delivery, whether that's in terms of dots per inch, video resolution and speed, or audio samples per second. These discrepancies will inevitably diminish in time.

So when should I use them?

Online media can only be used when learners have access to a workable Internet connection when they are learning, whether that's at work, at home or on the move. Even with good connectivity, there will be times when the online experience is simply not good enough and the traditional options will be preferable. However cheap and accessible it may be, online is not always enough.

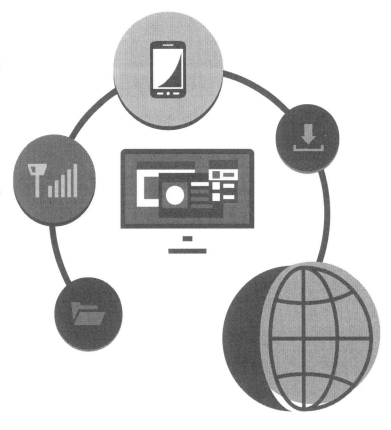

SUMMARY

	Face-to-face learning	*Offline media*	*Online media*
Advantages	Face-to-face learning is multi-sensory, going beyond sight and sound. Body language is easily visible. Learners can see and interact with the physical world. Face-to-face experiences are more intense and more memorable.	Offline media can be of very high quality, because quality is not constrained by internet bandwidth. Offline media are portable and easy to use. No internet connection is required. All offline media are asynchronous, which provides the learner with a lot of flexibility in terms of when and where they learn.	Online media frees the learner from the constraints of geographic location. Online media can be both synchronous and asynchronous, providing tremendous opportunities for blended solutions. Online content is easier to maintain because there is only one copy that everyone accesses. There are no practical limits to the amount of content that can be accessed online or the number of people that can access it.

	Face-to-face learning	Offline media	Online media
Disadvantages	All face-to-face learning is synchronous, which is less flexible and allows little space for reflection. To participate in face-to-face learning activities, learners may have to travel to a central location, which is time-consuming and expensive.	Offline content is less accessible because it has to be physically shipped or downloaded. Offline content is harder to maintain because whenever a change is made, every copy must be replaced. There are limits to how much offline content can be stored by the learner, whether physically or digitally. Physical offline media (books, CDs, DVDs) are more expensive to produce than their online equivalents.	The learner must have an internet connection and, to interact with audio and video, this connection must be of high bandwidth. Online media (and offline media too) do not provide as rich a multi-sensory experience as being face to face.

BLENDING BY COMMUNICATION MODE

OVERVIEW

Each learning medium operates in one of two different modes. Synchronous (or 'same-time') communication requires that all parties be available at the same time. Asynchronous (or 'own-time') communication can be undertaken as and when it suits the participants.

Same-time communication

All teaching originally took place face to face, and this form of communication is essentially synchronous – everyone needs to be available at the same time. Technology has expanded our capacity for same-time communication, first through the telephone and now using tools like Skype on the Internet. As a means for learning, synchronous events provide a more immediate and responsive experience but at the expense of flexibility for individual learners.

Own-time communication

Since the days of the printing press, it has been possible for large numbers of people to learn as it suits them, without having to fix dates in the diary with other people. More recently, discs and tapes expanded the possibilities for self-study by bringing audio and video into the mix. But asynchronous communication is about more than

consuming media – PCs and mobile devices allow us to interact with each other as and when we like, using options such as email and SMS messaging. The implications for learning are great – a more reflective and low-stress experience that you can schedule around your other commitments.

Putting these to use

> # As the most flexible option, asynchronous communication is likely to form the main part of many blended solutions.

However, synchronous events add immediacy and structure to an intervention, so a balance will often be desirable.

SAME-TIME COMMUNICATION

So what is it?

Same-time communication requires all participants to be available at the same time, although not necessarily in the same place.

How about some examples?

Face-to-face communication is always synchronous. TV and radio, while not bi-directional, can also be regarded

as same-time, because they operate to a schedule and (without access to recording devices) you have to be there at the time a programme is broadcast to view or listen in.

The invention of the telephone provided the first possibility for person-to-person communication at a distance. With the Internet, we can add to this all sorts of conferencing systems from Skype to Microsoft Lync to WebEx. These systems perhaps provide the best opportunity we've had so far to replicate the face-to-face experience without the need for learners to travel to one place.

At the very high end, telepresence systems use high definition video and high quality audio to create a video conferencing experience that is almost as compelling as being in the same room. While these systems are expensive and require participants to gather in specially built studios, there is every reason to believe that one day they will be ubiquitous.

What are the advantages?

Synchronous communication allows for a free-flowing dialogue, something that is simply not going to happen by letter, email, in a forum or even on Twitter. Imagine trying to run a role-play using any of these media!

In a same-time context, you have the potential to get quick answers to your questions and immediate feedback on your performance.

This level of responsiveness can be important in some situations, such as learning to drive or to handle customer queries. Generally speaking, a synchronous approach gets the job done quickly, whereas it can take ages to resolve an issue while you wait for people to respond asynchronously.

Synchronous events can also have more emotional energy (sometimes negative as well as positive) than their asynchronous equivalents. Most of us would prefer to watch a big sporting occasion live rather than see the recording some time later, even if we do not know the outcome. There is something about experiencing an event as it happens in the company of our peers, whether that's face to face or online. And this upsurge of emotion is going to make a big difference in terms of what we remember.

In the context of a blend, live events have another advantage – they act as a milestone to encourage learners to get the asynchronous work done. In a course which has no timetable, it is inevitable that individual study will be put off to a later date – after all, learning is rarely the most urgent task on our to do lists. Even if deadlines are established for asynchronous work, there is always the feeling that these could easily be pushed back if required.

However, when the course is punctuated with live events, such as workshops, conference calls or webinars, there is a massive incentive to get on with your 'homework' – no-one wants to be the one who hasn't got their work done.

And the disadvantages?

Same-time communication is inherently more stressful, because the learner is not able to control the pace. While the implication of too slow a pace may just be boredom, if the event is moving too fast this could cause cognitive overload, perhaps even panic. We know learners like to learn at their own pace and, while they are prepared to compromise this facility for the relative excitement of a live event, they do not want to do this on a long-term basis.

The primary disadvantage of synchronous communication is that it requires us to coordinate dates and times with others. Just think how difficult it can be to get hold of someone by phone, then think what it takes to get 20 people booked on to a webinar. Time zones also come into play – a webinar for a worldwide audience requires those in the West to get up before dawn and those in the East to log on well into the evening.

So when should I use it?

Some learning activities simply have to be synchronous, because learners require quick feedback or there is a need for a free-flowing discussion. Otherwise you might choose this mode of communication because you want to up the level of emotional engagement or simply to indicate a milestone in what is otherwise a self-paced learning intervention.

OWN-TIME COMMUNICATION

So what is it?

Asynchronous, or own-time communication does not tie the parties to any particular time, date or location. Communication takes place as and when it suits those involved.

How about some more examples?

As soon as we could draw, write or even leave a mark, humans found ways to communicate with others who were not right there with them at the same time.

However, the scope of this communication was limited by the fact that our messages could not easily be reproduced.

The advent of printing made it possible to share the written word with large numbers of people without the constraints of time and space, and this one development in technology was responsible for a huge upsurge in learning. In the twentieth century we added the capacity to record sound and video and distribute this on various forms of tape and disc; and CD-ROMs and game cartridges went a little further in that they allowed us to replicate and distribute interactive computer programmes.

The modern era has seen a dazzling array of new possibilities for self-paced consumption of content (think of Wikipedia, YouTube and millions of other web sites) and asynchronous person-to-person interaction, including text messaging on mobile devices, email, discussion forums, wikis, blogs and social networks.

What are the advantages?

Own-time communication provides the learner with the flexibility to learn at a time and pace that they choose, rather than at the convenience of some course provider. This makes self-study possible, with all the benefits that this bestows. It also allows learners to interact with tutors, co-learners and the wider community without having to make themselves available at a particular time. And learning in your own time is going to be of particular benefit to those who are studying part-time and have to juggle work and home commitments.

There are also benefits in terms of the quality of learning. Same-time communication leaves little room for reflection, which in many cases is an essential element in the learning process. While reflection benefits all learners, some people dislike the need for an instant response that is so prevalent in a live session and enjoy the ability to compose their responses with care over time. Having an own-time element will make sure that all learners get to communicate in the manner they prefer.

And the disadvantages?

Own-time learning does not have the urgency of same-time nor, without careful design, will it generate the same emotional response. Challenging activities will help as will storytelling with characters and situations to which the learner can easily relate, but you won't generate quite the same effect as 'being there' along with your peers when the event actually happens.

The lack of urgency inherent in own-time communication can lead to procrastination, as learners keep putting off their tasks to another day.

Only the most self-disciplined learners will get down to what are often seen as optional tasks without deadlines

and even then there are no guarantees. It's nice to have flexibility, but this can be overdone. Own-time learning works best within boundaries so, while you may have the flexibility to complete a task within a given period, you still have to adhere to the schedule for the programme as a whole.

Another difficulty can arise when managers do not allow their reports to take advantage of the flexibility inherent in own-time learning. You might publish a series of bite-sized modules, but managers may ask their staff to sit in front of a PC and do them all in one two-hour sitting – just because it makes it easier for them to manage their staff rota.

So when should I use it?
There should probably be an asynchronous element in every blend because, without this, learners will not have adequate opportunities for reflection. Own-time communication provides the flexibility that many learners are looking for, with the caveat that some same-time elements may be necessary to provide the impetus to get the own-time learning done.

SUMMARY

	Same-time communication	*Own-time communication*
Advantages	Allows for a free-flowing dialogue.	Provides the learner with greater flexibility over when they learn and at what pace.
	The learner gets a quick answer to their questions and speedy feedback on their performance.	Allows time for reflective learning.
	Live events have more energy and generate more of an emotional response.	
	They also act as milestones, encouraging learners to get their 'own-time' work done.	
Disadvantages	The learner may feel more stressed when they cannot control the pace.	Requires compelling activities and resources to generate the same emotional response.
	Same-time events are hard to coordinate, particularly over different time zones.	Easy to put off to another day.

A COMPENDIUM OF LEARNING MEDIA

The decisions you make about how you will deliver your chosen blended learning strategy are multi-faceted. You have a lot to consider:

- If there are to be face-to-face sessions, then where will these will take place and with the aid of what equipment?

- If there is an element to the learning that is not face to face, then where will that take place and with the aid of what equipment?

- In which formats will learning materials be delivered?

- In which ways will remote communication take place?

This compendium explores the options available at the time of writing for each of the above. While options in terms of spaces stay much the same, hardware and media formats are constantly evolving, so this is a compendium that could soon look out-dated.

SPACES FOR TEACHING AND LEARNING

Teaching

	What has this space got going for it?
The classroom	Apart from the fact that a classroom provides a convenient way to keep children out of their parents' hair for long periods, it does have some learning benefits too.
	In a work context, the classroom scores because it is away from the job, providing some hope of a respite from the usual constant interruptions. Having said that, whatever advantage there once was is being eroded as learners choose to bring mobile devices and laptops into the classroom.
	The classroom is a versatile space, easily adapted to different teaching and learning strategies. Set it up in theatre style for exposition, in a U-shape for instruction, in cabaret style for guided discovery? It is not quite that simple of course but you get the idea.
	The classroom has some disadvantages too. For one thing it has painful associations for all those learners who did not enjoy school. It also encourages the same teacher-pupil authority relationship that pervaded school life.
	In a vocational learning context, the major disadvantage of the classroom is that it is not the environment in which work takes place (unless you're a teacher!). It is easier to recall knowledge or apply skills in the same environment in which that knowledge and skill was originally learned.
A computer classroom	Computer classrooms are normal classrooms kitted out with lots of computers. These environments are obviously useful for IT training. Some organisations also use them as spaces for self-study learning, with someone on hand to deal with questions.

	What has this space got going for it?
A workshop	Be careful, because the word 'workshop' here means a building or room that houses the equipment needed to carry out some skilled manual task, rather than a classroom session focusing on practical work.
	A workshop is an ideal environment in which to learn a skilled manual trade. While the environment is not as authentic as being on the job, it is close.
	Because the amount of equipment in a workshop is limited and often expensive, learners will have only limited time in which to practise. For this reason, we should be pleased to see the recent development of simulators based on low-cost computers, which allow learners to practise skills such as plumbing and electrical work to their heart's content.
A lecture theatre / conference hall	A lecture theatre or conference hall is ideally suited to exposition to relatively large audiences. However, lectures and presentations can now be delivered online to much larger audiences and recorded for the benefit of wider audiences still.
	The investment required to provide a face-to-face experience to a few hundred people is enormous compared with the cost of reaching thousands, perhaps millions, online. Unless the speaker is a star performer whose presence alone bestows a unique privilege on his or her audience, the real benefit of these environments may well be the facility they provide for networking before and after the session.
On the job with an instructor	The job environment has one major advantage – you will be learning in exactly the same situation in which you will be performing, While the job environment is authentic and well suited to one-to-one instruction, there are the obvious dangers of noise and continual interruptions.
In a simulator room with an instructor	Not many of us have the luxury of using equipment costing millions that has the sole purpose of allowing us to practise our skills safely, but airline pilots, tube train drivers and the like certainly do.
	The benefits of simulators in reducing accidents and other unwelcome outcomes are well documented. The millions are spent to make the experience entirely authentic, and if you combine an authentic environment with masses of opportunities for practice, with feedback available from skilled instructors, you will obtain highly skilled practitioners as a result.

	What has this space got going for it?
On a visit	Visits allow people the opportunity to see how things are done somewhere other than where they normally work. A visit to a department or organisation upon which you depend to provide input to your work, or which in turn depends on you in the same way, provides a great opportunity to gain insights and resolve problems. A visit to a department or organisation that does similar work to you provides an opportunity for sharing ideas and comparing experiences.
In the great outdoors	For some, such as park wardens, gardeners, mountaineers and rugby players, the outdoors is equivalent to being on the job. For others, typically office-based employees developing their leadership skills and their teamwork, this is certainly not an authentic environment in which to practise. Whether outdoor learning experiences deliver results depends on how well they are designed and facilitated, and the extent to which you believe that the insights employees achieve rock climbing and crossing lakes can be transferred back to the day job.

Learning

Of course, most learning does not happen face to face with a teacher or instructor present. So in what other environments can learning take place and which are most conducive to learning?

	What has this space got going for it?
On the job	Survey after survey tells us that learners like most to learn on the job, whatever that environment might be. Experiential and social learning will happen regardless of any formal planning, but you can accelerate the process by making it as easy as possible for novices to observe and learn from their more experienced colleagues and to network with their peers.
At a desk	For knowledge workers, the desk is the job environment, but let's consider it here as a special case with self-study and collaborative distance learning in mind.

The main difficulty with an office environment is the danger of constant interruptions by telephone, email, instant messaging or people just turning up. Some learners may be able to put up the shutters and concentrate for prolonged periods, but many more will find this impossible.

If you are creating learning materials for use at the desktop, keep them short and to the point, or at least make them available in small pieces. And, if the materials include audio, make sure you supply learners with headphones. |
| In a learning centre or pod | Taking the theme of self-study and collaborative distance learning a little further, some organisations create special spaces just for this purpose, free from interruptions. For extended periods of study, let's say half an hour or more, this may be your best option. |
| At home | While no employer should simply expect employees to learn at home, unless perhaps they are engaged on a course of self-development of their own choosing, for some people the home provides the best opportunity to get some quality time. Home PCs are usually much more powerful than the ones used at work and with better bandwidth, and you will not be constrained as to what software you can use.

However, be mindful of the fact that not everyone has a peaceful home to go back to and that you might have to go to special lengths to ensure that your organisation's learning platforms and materials will be available over the Internet. |

	What has this space got going for it?
On the move	Increasingly, people carry their computers in their pockets, rucksacks, handbags or on their wrist. And, as is evident in any public place, they refer to them almost constantly.
	Trains, planes, airports and hotel rooms provide people with a perfect environment in which to concentrate on a task, and a learning assignment that has otherwise been put on the back burner may well get picked up when there is dead time to fill.

HARDWARE FOR TEACHING AND LEARNING

Within teaching and learning spaces, all sorts of hardware can be employed:

Teaching

	What function does this hardware perform?
Writing and drawing devices (blackboards, whiteboards, flip charts, interactive whiteboards)	You will find one or more of these devices in just about every classroom in the world. They make it possible for teachers and learners to make impromptu notes and drawings, and to record the outcomes from group activities.
	Electronic whiteboards go further in that they combine these functions with those of the projected computer display (see below), making it much easier to save and distribute what is written or drawn. While these seem attractive features, interactive whiteboards have not taken off as expected and many learners are happier just to take photographs of flip charts and whiteboards with their smart phones.
Dedicated video playback devices (videocassette players, DVD players, film projectors)	While flip charts and whiteboards remain, most dedicated audio-visual playback devices have been replaced by computers that can do everything that these devices do and much more.
Slide projectors (overhead, 35mm)	As above. If you are still using slide projectors, why?

	What function does this hardware perform?
Projected computer displays	Computers have taken over the roles once played by video players and slide projectors, but they are capable of a lot more, for example: displaying websites, documents and online movies; delivering quizzes, scenarios, games, Twitter feeds and other interactive experiences; using web conferencing to bring in guest speakers and other groups from remote locations.
Video cameras	Video cameras have long been used to record role-plays and other practical exercises. The advantage now is that video cameras, whether stand alone or built into mobile devices, are practically ubiquitous (although you'll still need a tripod for a steady picture) and the results can be easily stored and played back on a laptop.

Learning

	What function does this hardware perform?
TVs and radios	Of course we all learn incidentally from broadcast media, but their place as a formal learning delivery medium has been almost entirely replaced by personal computing devices.
Audio and video players (tape/disc/solid state)	Again, this sort of equipment is here largely for historical interest. Perhaps iPods and the like still have a role to play, but then they're really computers.
Landline telephones	Just to complete the set of almost irrelevant learning devices, we must not forget the landline. Handy for phoning your tutor or getting technical support, except nowadays you're going to do that online, aren't you?
Personal computers	Windows, Mac or Chromebooks, these devices can pretty well do it all, assuming a good Internet connection (or, for the unlucky few that don't, a CD/DVD player). With full-size keyboards, mice, large screens and huge amounts of storage, PCs are perfect for active learning assignments that involve writing, editing images, audio and video, or assembling spreadsheets and presentations.
Tablet computers	Tablets are less versatile than PCs but in some ways more conducive to learning. They're more portable than laptop PCs, more easy to use, they allow you to concentrate on one thing at a time and, perhaps most importantly, you don't associate them with work.
	Tablets may not be as great for creative learning assignments lacking, as they do, a proper keyboard and with limited multi-tasking, but then it's easy enough to attach a Bluetooth keyboard if you need one, and the ability to interact with several apps at the same time will soon be commonplace.

	What function does this hardware perform?
Smart phones	Almost everyone has one and they can do everything a tablet can do but with a smaller screen. While it is unusual for people to engage with complex content on a smartphone, they will watch videos and slideshows, keep up-to-date with emails, course forums and the like, and maybe participate in a virtual classroom or webinar.
E-book readers	E-book readers are purpose designed for reading and work well in all conditions, including bright sunlight. For magazines and books that are heavily graphical, a tablet will work better. For courses that involve a great deal of reading, e-book readers could be ideal.
Games consoles	Games are highly interactive and amazingly addictive. Any computer can be used for games, but consoles such as the Nintendo Wii or Xbox Kinect have the advantage of add-on controllers that enable convincing simulations of physical tasks.
Virtual reality headsets	Although intended primarily to enhance video gameplay, headsets such as the soon-to-arrive Oculus Rift, which allows for an immersive 360-degree 3D experience, will provide opportunities for all manners of simulation.
Augmented reality devices	Augmented reality superimposes computer-generated information on what a user is seeing of the world around them. A good example is Google Glass, a wearable computer with an optical, head-mounted display. One of the principal learning applications of augmented reality is to provide location-sensitive information as a form of performance support or to enhance the learning experience in places such as museums.

MEDIA FORMATS

Asynchronous offline

	What is it?	*How can it help learning?*
The printed page	We all know what this is and the range of forms that it can take, from posters to books to newspapers and magazines.	We are all comfortable learning from the printed page and we can take printed materials just about anywhere. However, there are limits to how much paper we can practically store and carry with us. As a result, we are quickly substituting online and downloaded media such as e-books.
Recordable audio-visual media	Humans have found all sorts of ingenious ways to store audio and visual material on discs and tapes, originally in analogue format and then digital.	There is still some potential for distributing audio-visual material on CDs and DVDs, for those people that do not yet have good Internet access. However, the days of these recordable media are fast disappearing.
Downloaded audio and video	CDs and DVDs have now largely been replaced by downloaded media files, including music, podcasts, movies and shorter videos. While the user has to be online to do the downloading, they need no Internet connection to play the recordings.	Downloaded media are a good solution for learners who have access to a good Internet connection but want to be able to play back material when they are offline, perhaps on a train or plane.
E-book	An e-book is a digital text and graphics resource that can be read from a dedicated e-book reader (such as a Kindle) or on some other form of computer. These devices can easily store many thousands of books.	E-books provide a very convenient way to share large volumes of textual material with learners who want to be able to continue reading when they are not online.

	What is it?	*How can it help learning?*
Downloaded document	Many popular types of document, including Word files, Excel spreadsheets, PowerPoint files and PDFs, are intended primarily for offline use and must be downloaded.	Microsoft Office documents can prove a useful resource, particularly if learners need to be able to make modifications to them, as they would with a template.
		PDFs are useful because they allow for high-quality printing, should learners require this.
Single player video game	Video games come in many formats – adventure, action, strategy, quiz, etc. They run on dedicated games consoles as well as just about any other type of computer.	As we all know, video games are capable of eating up endless hours of our time, but this time can be productively spent if the content of the game is of educational value or the skills needed to be successful in the game can be applied in other contexts.
Single player 3D world	Allows a user to navigate a 3D world and interact with objects and computer-generated characters.	This format is being used extensively by the military and others to provide learners with opportunities to explore and practise skills in an authentic environment.
		With the aid of special input devices, virtual reality helmets and other add-ons, the 3D world can be extended into a full-scale simulator.
Mobile app	An app is a software application for a mobile device such as a smartphone or tablet. Many apps require Internet access to function, but others will happily run offline, including most games.	Offline apps provide a useful way to support learners with reference information and decision aids, even when no Internet connection is available.
		They could also be used to deliver e-learning modules and other interactive multimedia material.

Synchronous offline

	What is it?	*How can it help learning?*
TV or radio broadcast	Live transmission of radio and TV	Has been used historically as a way of delivering programmes to a learner's home (e.g. the Open University). In a learning context these have now largely been replaced by online and recorded media.
Telephone conversation	Use of the telephone network for voice communications	A useful alternative to online media for coaching sessions, technical support and small group meetings.

Asynchronous online

	What is it?	*How can it help learning?*
Web page	Scrolling pages of text and graphics, often including means for interaction such as forms and links between pages; delivered through a web browser (Internet Explorer, Chrome, Safari, Firefox, etc.). Web pages are formatted using Hypertext Markup Language (HTML), often enriched with sophisticated scripting languages.	A highly flexible and versatile way to deliver learning content to any sort of computing device. Web pages are the basis for much e-learning and many of the other asynchronous online formats listed below.
Flash movie	Originally developed as a way to add animation capability to web pages but has been extended over the years to provide rich multimedia and interactive capabilities. Usually hosted by a web page but can run independently. A proprietary format (currently owned by Adobe) but the player is free.	Historically, a great deal of e-learning has been delivered using Flash. However, because Flash is not supported on mobile devices, it is quickly being replaced by the more widely compatible (but, as yet, less powerful) HTML5.

	What is it?	*How can it help learning?*
Forum	Allows a user to post a question or proposition and for others to then reply with an answer or counter-argument, etc. Discussions can become protracted as more people get involved and the dialogue moves back and forth.	Forums are an almost essential component of most distance learning courses, providing a simple way for learners to collaborate in their own time and to keep a record of that conversation.
Blog	Usually established by an individual (but occasionally an organisation) as a means for making regular postings reflecting on current thoughts and experiences. Blogs have very similar characteristics to columns in newspapers and magazines. Readers can reply to blog postings.	The process of blogging can be a highly productive learning experience because it compels the blogger to reflect on their experiences and construct meaning. In the context of a course, a blog can act as a learning journal, shared only with the learning group.
Wiki	A wiki is a network of web pages, the content of which is created by users. The most obvious example is Wikipedia.	Wikis can be used as a means for learning groups to collaborate on developing a shared output. They can also allow the work of one group to be shared with future groups.
Social network	Allows large numbers of people to interconnect as networks of 'friends' or as groups to share experiences, chat, share media such as videos and photos, play games, etc. Obvious examples are Facebook and LinkedIn.	Much informal learning takes place through the social networks that people use every day. Learners can set up groups in social networks to support the courses they are on. Many employers have private social networks operating within their firewalls. Virtual learning environments (VLE) and learning management systems (LMS) often now include social networking functionality.

	What is it?	*How can it help learning?*
Microblogging	Allows individuals to provide short status updates, make comments, share resources, etc. with others who have decided to follow them. The most obvious example is Twitter, although Yammer is also widely used within organisations.	Microblogging will often provide people with access to information and resources that they would otherwise never discover. It can also be used to create a free flow of ideas around a topic, including a conference or classroom session.
Streamed audio and video	Allows users to watch videos or listen to audio programmes without having to download these to their devices. The most obvious examples are YouTube and Netflix for movies and Spotify for music.	Streaming media provide the most flexible and convenient means for providing access to audio and video material for learners who have access to a good Internet connection.

Synchronous online

	What is it?	*How can it help learning?*
Instant messaging	The real-time exchange of text messages between two or more people. It can be extended to include audio and video (see Internet telephony below).	Allows impromptu exchanges between a learner and a teacher or subject expert, perhaps through a learning management system. Provides a useful means for obtaining technical support. Allows for quick exchanges between learners.
Voice Over IP, e.g. Skype	A facility for voice and video calls between two or more people.	Skype and similar programs provide a useful way to hold coaching conversations. Also useful for meetings of small groups of learners.

	What is it?	*How can it help learning?*
Web conferencing	A facility for virtual meetings, presentations and classroom sessions. Will usually include voice and video communication, text chat, polling, application sharing, media playback, slide presentations and electronic whiteboards. Meetings can be recorded.	Live group sessions, avoiding the need for learners to travel. Particularly suitable for shorter (1–2 hour) sessions. Makes it easier to bring in guest speakers from remote locations. Will support very large groups.
Real-time 3D worlds	3D environments in which people can navigate a virtual world and communicate with each other, e.g. Second Life or multi-player video games.	After a lot of initial hype, this medium has not yet proved to be particularly valuable for learning, although game players can undoubtedly learn a great deal of value indirectly. 3D worlds show considerable promise as environments providing opportunities for realistic practice of major incidents for the military, hospitals, fire and police, etc.

ONLINE AND OWN-TIME

— THE NEW DEFAULT POSITION

The default means of delivery for teaching and training for hundreds, if not thousands of years has been face to face. As a result, it is extremely tempting when faced with making a decision on a solution to assume, as a starting position, that it should be face to face. But face-to-face learning, while sometimes powerful, can also be expensive[18], is inflexible and hard to scale.

So why not start with what is usually the least expensive, most flexible and most scalable solution and see first of all if that will do the job? Could your learning solution be delivered online and in the learner's own time, using web resources and social media such as discussion forums?

18_ *Clearly, face-to-face learning will not always be the most expensive option. When everyone shares the same physical space, perhaps because they work on the same site, there will be no additional travel and accommodation costs.*

If this really does not work, at least
for all of your solution, then consider
next whether some elements should
be same-time. Would your programme
benefit from opportunities for learners
to interact with each other and with
facilitators in real time? If so, don't
assume this has to be face to face.
Think carefully about whether a virtual
classroom would do the job.

If you are absolutely sure that learners need to be in the same physical space, then fine – go ahead.

At least you will be choosing what is
often the most expensive, least flexible
and least scalable solution for the right
reason – not because that is how you
have always done things in the past,
but because it is the only way to
guarantee quality.

THE

BL

COLLECTION:

INITIATIVE

TRANS-
FORMING
SOFTWARE
USAGE

AT INITIATIVE

This project shows how, by taking a blended approach, what could have been seen as a simple IT training exercise has resulted in a transformation in the usage of a key software tool.

TALKING ABOUT
THE MATRIX PROGRAMME

Geoff Copps,
Research Director, IPG Mediabrands UK

Initiative is a media agency, forming part of the IPG Mediabrands global network, and operating in over 75 markets across the world. Initiative has a market-leading tool that offers planning insights for all of our clients, but with that strength comes a challenge. The tool is very complex so we need to disseminate knowledge about the tool across the business and make sure it's working as effectively as possible for our clients.

In terms of learning about the tool, there were two aspects that we needed to cover. The first was hard knowledge on how to use the tool to get the most effective usage of clients' media budgets. The second was about encouraging clients to

love it, for it to become part of the culture of the agency and ultimately become embedded within daily working practices.

Initiative employs over two and a half thousand people across the globe. The key audience for this programme was the planners. These are the people who work day-to-day with our clients to help them optimise and use their budget most effectively. They are a diverse bunch, varied in age and in their level of experience but, most importantly perhaps, they are time poor. They've got lots else on their plate. We were looking for a solution that would cut through all that.

Lisa Minogue-White,
Director of Learning Solutions, Willow DNA

We were approached by Initiative to develop this solution predominantly off the back of our work with the IPA, the professional body for advertising media,

an industry which has a particular culture and particular demands. We needed to make sure that whatever solution we developed reflected that for it to be credible.

The way in which learners come to the system is slightly unusual but for us very interesting, because it marries the informal and formal. There was a Yammer community that already existed for this tool. Initiative only has a small number of very highly expert users of the system and this community was a place people could come to and ask them questions.

Of course the experts are thinly spread over a large organisation, so what Initiative wanted was that, when learners came into the community, they were also offered the opportunity to take part in a formal learning programme. It gave them all that good stuff that they would have got from those experts in a timely fashion. It's chunked up in a way that they can access the learning at a time that suits them, given they are extremely time poor.

People can do the formal learning programme then feed their experience back into the community. You then have that virtuous loop of learning.

The formal learning itself is blended but it's simple and it's chunked up. We use e-learning to set the scene. We then use walkthroughs with voiceover to help people contextualise how they will use the tool. We support that with case studies in which people can see how Matrix has contributed to real pitches. Then we use assignments so learners can provide evidence of the way in which they're using the tool in their working lives.

We introduced discussions into the formal learning to get people to embody good learning behaviours. Once they finish the programme, they can continue to contribute back into the Yammer community. It was quite an interesting design: keep it simple, chunk it up in a useful way but try to keep that loop of learning going.

Application back into the workplace was an interesting challenge. One of the ways we achieved this was by trying to contextualise as many of the walkthroughs as possible by linking to the types of real conversations and pitches that learners would be involved in. We have videos shot in different Initiative locations around the world with people talking about their local context. Without that, it may not have felt as if people could apply what they had learned as readily to their working life.

The real big win was the case study competition that occurs at the end of the formal programme. When a group of learners has completed the formal learning, the office is asked to submit a case study to demonstrate exactly how what they have learned has informed and affected the way in which they pitch to a client. This directly links learning with business outcomes and some of the figures are very impressive indeed.

An absolutely crucial takeaway from a programme like this is that it needs facilitation.

To avoid isolation of learners, to make them feel that they're part of a shared experience, you need somebody that cares.

More important is keeping the formal content contemporary, lively and alive. So your facilitator is able to curate from the discussion board, the learners' assignments and the case study competitions and put that into the formal learning. It keeps it all very fresh.

One of the core design principles of the programme was to ensure it wasn't just a course that people took for a period of time, that they finish and then walk away; it also had to be designed as a performance support tool. The way in which we chunked up the learning means that people can dip back in right before a pitch to a client, get the information that they need, jump back out, refreshed, and then be able to use that for maximum effect with their clients.

Joanna Foyle, community facilitator

Since we launched the programme, planners are much more interested and engaged in training. The UK team used a 'wall of fame' to track people's progress and now it has achieved 100% completion for the entire team.

Previously, people rarely talked about Matrix. Now there is dialogue every day. Understanding how learning works and placing the learning within the community has made such a difference.

Geoff Copps

The outcome from the programme has been excellent. Engagement with the tool has really surged and it's helped inform our pitch work and our response to briefs for clients. On the softer side, our planners have really learned to love the tool and continually communicate that enthusiasm and those insights to our clients.

WHAT PARTICIPANTS HAVE TO SAY

Enrico Girotti, Italy

When I first accessed the e-learning platform, I thought it would be an effective support in helping people use the Matrix tool, but I was wrong. It's super effective.

Rita Martins, Portugal

Very clear and user friendly. It's been a great help for both initial and more experienced users. The videos helped to put Matrix in context. It's really important for users to see the value of Matrix behind the technical perspective.

Paola Cassone, Netherlands

Awesome! I am addicted to it already! I need to remember I've got a home to go back to tonight.

ANALYSED: LEARNING TO LOVE THE MATRIX TOOL

The situation

The need	Initiative has a market-leading tool that offers media planning insights for its clients. However that tool is complex and was not being applied as effectively as it could.
The learning	Initiative were looking for two key outcomes: (1) technical knowledge in using the Matrix tool and (2) a passion for the tool that would lead to its everyday use.
The learners	The programme was aimed primarily at media planners. These are varied in age and experience, and time poor.
The logistics	Initiative's 2,500 employees are distributed across 90 offices in 75 markets. Most speak English as a second language.

The blend

	Methods	*Media*
Preparation	Planners are introduced to the programme through their Yammer community.	Online
Input	Software walkthroughs, video interviews, case studies of Matrix usage and discussions with other learners.	Online through the portal
Application	Assignments in which learners provide evidence of how they are using Matrix.	Online through the portal
	Case study competition.	Submitted online
Follow-up	Planners have access to the programme materials on a performance support basis.	Online through the portal
	Planners continue to engage through the Yammer community.	Online

PART 7
IMPLEMENTATION

MAKING THE CASE FOR BLENDED SOLUTIONS

COMING TO TERMS WITH BLENDED LEARNING

The most widespread understanding of blended learning is as a mix of face-to-face and online delivery within a learning intervention, what we have described in this book as a blend of delivery channels. Using this simple definition, a typical blend might combine something face to face – perhaps a workshop or some on-job instruction – with something online – maybe some e-content or web conferencing.

The argument for blending delivery channels is that, in many circumstances, it is difficult, if not impossible, to optimise outcomes through the use of a single learning medium – a mix will do the job better. There simply isn't one channel that works in all circumstances, just as there is not a single tool that will work for all forms of DIY or a single software application that can be used for all office tasks.

The research from academia backs up the idea that a combination of face-to-face and online learning works better than a single medium:

- Blended learning can improve learning outcomes (studies conducted at the University of Tennessee and Stanford University).

- Students are very positive about blended learning (Sharpe et al 2006).

- Blended learning produces a stronger sense of community among students (Rovai and Jordan 2004).

- Blended learning improves students' interaction and overall satisfaction (DeLacey and Leonard 2002).

- Blended learning maximises the advantages of both face-to-face and online learning (Schlager et al 2002).

- Blended learning improves students' satisfaction (Dziuban et al, 2004; Wingard 2004).

- Blended learning improves the interaction between peers and instructors (Chamberlin and Moon 2005).

- Students who took all or part of their instruction online performed better, on average, than those taking the same course through face-to-face instruction. Further, those who took blended courses appeared to do best of all (meta-analysis conducted by the U.S. Department of Education, 2010).

Workplace surveys yield similarly positive results:

- A structured curriculum of blended learning generated a 30 per cent increase in accuracy of performance and a 41 per cent increase in speed of performance over single-delivery options (NETg survey, 2003).

- For 89% of employees, blended learning is living up to users' expectations 'well' or 'very well' (CEGOS survey of 2355 employees across Europe, 2009).

- Some 86% of respondents are blending frequently or sometimes. Of these, 54% are reporting improvements in business performance (report from Kineo and The Oxford Group, 2013).

This is useful evidence but it does not provide a clear picture of *why* it is that blended learning works. As research from Sitzmann and Wisher (2006) has established, the medium has a relatively insignificant influence on learning effectiveness. It is the *methods* that you use which will determine whether an intervention delivers against its objectives; the choice of *media*, on the other hand, helps to optimise efficiency (the use of resources, such as time, money, equipment and facilities) as well as providing employers and learners with improved flexibility in how, where and when learning can take place.

When you mix face-to-face and online learning, you are doing much more than just shifting the medium. You are highly likely to be using the two approaches for very different purposes. For example, you may use online learning for self-study and the classroom for practical group activities. The mix of different methods (self-study and group activities) is much more likely to be making the difference in terms of learning effectiveness than the combination of two delivery channels.

If you want to enhance the *effectiveness* of a learning intervention, then you are more likely to blend the social context (individual, one-to-one, group or community learning) or the learning strategy (exposition, instruction, guided discovery, exploration) than you are the medium.

Once you have established the right mix of strategies and social contexts for learning, you can then divert your attention to selecting the learning media that will allow all this to happen as efficiently as possible. Although, in most cases, a mix of media will work best, it is also conceivable that a single medium will work for every element of your blend. In other words,

---

it is possible that a really effective blend could be implemented entirely online or entirely face to face.

As a result, I have endeavoured, in this book, to put forward a much broader definition. In its most elaborate form it could be expressed as follows:

A blended learning solution mixes social contexts for learning (self-study, one-to-one, small group, wider community) and different learning strategies with the aim of increasing learning effectiveness. It may also mix delivery channels (face-to-face, offline media, synchronous and asynchronous online media, etc.) to increase efficiency and flexibility. These choices will be made in the context of a particular learning requirement, audience characteristics, and practical constraints and opportunities.

More succinctly, a blended solution could be defined as an intervention that combines contrasting methods and/or media in order to optimise effectiveness and efficiency.

WHEN BLENDING PAYS OFF

The argument for blended learning is really very simple. Each of the most common approaches to learning and development has its own distinct advantages and disadvantages. Consider the examples of face-to-face workshops, one-to-one coaching sessions and online self-study content – each is capable of both contributing to the effectiveness of a learning intervention and of getting in the way. Each has its efficiencies and its inefficiencies.

In some situations, given the particular learning requirements, audience characteristics and practical constraints and opportunities, the disadvantages are not significant and can be tolerated. In others cases, the compromise is too great and the solution becomes unsatisfactory – only a blend of approaches will achieve the learning effectiveness that you require, while making efficient use of available resources, such as time, budget, skills, tools, equipment and facilities.

So what are those situations? Generally speaking, a blended approach is *most* likely to be appropriate in the following circumstances:

The learning requirement is complex and multi-faceted: You are much less likely to blend if all your learning objectives are of a single class – knowledge and information, cognitive skills, interpersonal skills, motor skills, big ideas, etc. Conversely, when your objectives are wide-ranging, it could be really hard to find a single approach that will address them all satisfactorily. For example, in an induction programme for telephone call centre operators, you may need to provide product knowledge, IT skills, the ability to interact effectively with the customer, as well as selling in some big ideas about the importance of the customer to the business. It would be hard to address all these different types of learning effectively using a single approach.

You need to provide an end-to-end solution: As we have seen from the examples presented in this book, the best blends provide an end-to-end experience, from Preparation, through Input and Application to Follow-up. Take a typical training task, in which you want someone to develop a skill and apply this on the job. This is likely to involve engaging the learner and providing some background knowledge, such as facts, concepts and principles; it may demand that you demonstrate the skill in question; you may want to provide an opportunity for safe practice of the skill and then support the learner in their first attempts to use the skill in a live situation; ideally you will then continue to provide support as the learner develops mastery. Inevitably you will need a blend here as you move across the continuum from abstract to concrete, from theory to practice.

The learning need is sizeable and the intervention is therefore likely to be prolonged: Because there are more ingredients to be organised, blending comes at a price administratively, so you're less likely to create a blend for a one-hour intervention than you are for, say, a three-week induction or on-boarding programme. A blended solution will, almost by definition, offer more variety and therefore help to maintain interest.

The target audience is relatively heterogeneous in terms of their prior knowledge, motivation, preferences and other characteristics: Blended solutions lend themselves to a modular architecture, providing learners with more flexibility to mix and match the elements that meet their needs. You can also design some redundancy into a blend, so elements overlap to some degree in the content that they address. This allows learners some scope to concentrate on those elements that they find most helpful and/or most convenient in their particular circumstances. Blends can also be modified and extended while the intervention is in progress, in response to problems and opportunities that arise.

So, not every situation requires a blend, but a sizeable proportion does. It would be fair to say that a great many current learning interventions are attempting the impossible because they employ a single social context, strategy, delivery channel or communication mode, when this is clearly not versatile enough to do the job.

BLENDED LEARNING IS A CONTINUUM

Sometimes it seems that the more you think about blended solutions, the harder it is to define what is and what is not blended. This decision is complicated by the fact that there are so many aspects of a solution that you can choose to blend:

Learning methods:

- You can blend the social contexts in which the learning takes place
- You can blend the educational and training strategies that you use

Learning media:

- You can blend the delivery channel used to deliver your methods
- You can blend the communication mode to obtain a mix of same-time and own-time elements

I've reached the conclusion that blending is a continuum, from not blending at all at one extreme, through to very significant shifts in methods and media within a single solution. Let's look at some points upon this continuum, starting with the least blended:

1. You use a single method and medium throughout the intervention, e.g. reading from a book or face-to-face coaching.

2. You use a variety of methods but within a single social context and using a single delivery channel, for example: a classroom course with case studies, presentations, discussion, role-play; or an e-learning course including demos, simulations, quizzes.

3. You use a variety of methods, employing different social contexts, but still delivered through a single delivery channel, for example: within a face-to-face classroom course, you employ a mix of self-study, one-to-one coaching and group work; or within an online distance learning course, you use a mix of self-study, one-to-one support, collaboration through an online discussion forum and live online group sessions.

4. You use a variety of methods, employing different social contexts, but this time you use a variety of delivery channels as well, for example: a mix of face-to-face workshops, self-study with printed materials and CDs, online forum discussions and telephone tutor support.

Clearly number 1 in this list is not blended at all and number 4 is, from any perspective, but what about 2 and 3? They are blended in some respects but not others. And does it really matter whether a solution can be defined as blended or not? Surely the only important issue is whether it works.

It would be easy to argue that, with so little agreement on definitions, the concept of a blended solution is not actually that useful, but I can't accept that. So many solutions, particularly in workplace learning, employ a single approach throughout when this doesn't really deliver the results. The approach may work for some aspects of the solution but not for all.

A good example would be a stand-alone classroom workshop that attempts to deliver a body of knowledge, as well as provide opportunities for practice and discussion. The classroom may do a good job of the latter but not the former. And it ignores the fact that learning continues beyond the classroom and into the workplace, and this may need to be supported by coaching and reference materials.

The whole idea of blending is to use the right methods and media at each and every step in a solution, whether the elements are formal, informal, on-demand or experiential. That's very different to the traditional way we have addressed learning requirements.

PREPARING THE GROUND

BLENDED LEARNING, NO REGRETS

Adopting blended learning as a strategy is anything but business as usual. The ingredients that you intend to use in your blends may be familiar to you, your clients and your customers, but the process of blending may well be something new and may not, at first look, be welcomed by everyone involved.

To steel yourself to manage this process, it's a good idea to remind yourself why the change is necessary. Far too many learning interventions are seen as a diversion from the real job, in some cases a necessary chore, in others a welcome opportunity to get away from the routine. The deal has been a convenient one, from the perspective of both the middle manager and the learning professional[19]:

Far too many learning interventions are seen as a diversion from the real job, in some cases a necessary chore, in others a welcome opportunity to get away from the routine.

19_ *Charles Jennings introduced me to the idea of this deal between line managers and trainers: www.duntroom.com.*

I, the middle manager have people working for me with training and development needs; you, the learning professional can unburden me of this responsibility by 'processing' my people in some way so that the need is met; I can then enter a big tick on my to-do list; you can continue to do your thing with no questions asked by me (assuming good scores on the happy sheets).

Blended learning, at least the *more than* approach, breaks away from this cosy arrangement. It recognises the fact that learning is a journey, not an event. It works on the assumption that everyone benefits from learning interventions that deliver in terms of improved performance – not in a classroom, but on the job. To do this, it must blur the boundaries between learning that is formal, on-demand and experiential. And this process cannot occur in the black box that is the typical training event. It requires the on-going involvement of middle managers and the commitment of learners to do more than just turn up.

A blended solution starts on the job (the Preparation phase); it can include a wide range of possible learning activities (the Input phase); it ensures that new knowledge, skills and ideas are put to work back on the job (the Application phase); and it supports the learner as they continue their journey (the Follow-up phase).

WHAT'S DIFFERENT ABOUT BLENDED LEARNING?

Blended learning is different in some significant ways from the status quo. First of all, it is more complex to administer. It is relatively easy to schedule and monitor individual learning inputs – a single coaching session, a one-day workshop, an hour's e-learning. Most learning management systems assume that each of these elements is discrete and simply serve them up from a menu. On the other hand, a blended solution will contain a number of elements, some of which will have to be completed in sequence, some applied adaptively depending on the learner's progress, and some a matter of individual preference for the learner.

In some cases the blend will also depend on a single cohort of learners following through all of these elements together – a normal practice in an educational context but less usual for your typical corporate LMS[20]. It is not surprising therefore, that as blended learning has become more popular, employers have made increasing use of virtual learning environments (VLEs) such as Moodle or Blackboard, which were originally intended for educational use. The reason is simple enough – on the whole VLEs are better suited to blends involving cohorts of learners than most traditional LMSs.

We have already discussed the fact that blends place a greater demand on the middle manager. In the Preparation phase, the manager must engage with the learner, to agree goals and priorities. In the Application phase, they must support the learner in putting what they have learned into practice and then supply coaching support as necessary.

20_ *Although corporate learning management systems are used most of the time to provide access to stand-alone classroom events or e-learning packages, most are capable of handling blends. However, many administrators may not be aware of this functionality.*

Outsourcing specialists KnowledgePool conducted a study with input from more than 10,000 learners and their managers over a three-year period. The data was collected from an online survey issued three months after the completion of training, and focused on the degree to which the transfer of learning had taken place and the effect this had on performance. Their results are summarised in a downloadable white paper, *They Think It's All Over*. Here is one of the main findings:

"Line manager support to help learners use what they had learned was a major factor in tackling the lack of performance improvement. The study found that where learners did receive line manager support, 94 per cent went on to apply what they had learned, and performance improvement invariably followed."

The study found that where learners did receive line manager support, 94 per cent went on to apply what they had learned, and performance improvement invariably followed.

When assessing what made the biggest impact on transfer of learning, Broad and Newstrom[21] looked at three different parties – the learner's manager, the trainer/facilitator and the learner themselves – at three stages in the process – before the intervention, during and after. They found that the greatest impact was made by the learner's manager in setting expectations before the intervention; next most important was the trainer's role before the intervention in getting to know the needs of the learners they would be training; and third was the manager's role after the intervention.

So what's in it for middle managers? It's simple really. An end to the dishonesty of the previous arrangement in which training was seen to take place but nothing really happened. In its place, the very real prospect of more competent and confident employees; people who will carry out their duties more effectively and efficiently, and place less demands on you, the manager. As an added bonus, blended solutions are likely to involve shorter periods of time for learners away from the job and more flexible scheduling.

Blended learning also places new demands on the learner, who will have to be more self-reliant and more organised. It is, of course, much simpler to turn up at a classroom course on your allotted day, take as much part in the event as you feel appropriate, and then get on with your 'real' job as the whole experience vanishes inexorably from your memory. Simpler, but also incredibly frustrating. Many courses are genuinely inspiring and do have real application to your work. However, you are typically provided with little in the way of support or encouragement in following up on your new passions or cementing your new skills.

A well-designed blended learning experience provides the learner with more autonomy, a greater sense of purpose and a chance to achieve mastery – the three powerful motivators described in Daniel Pink's fabulous book *Drive*[22].

21_ *Transfer of Training by Mary L Broad and John W Newstrom, Basic Books (1992).*

22_ *Drive: The surprising truth about what motivates us by Daniel Pink, Canongate Books (2011).*

WITH BLENDING
COMES TECHNOLOGY

When the term 'blended learning' first came into popular use about 10 years ago, it was often used as a euphemism for e-learning. In the dotcom boom, self-study e-learning was over-hyped as a solution which could replace all 'traditional' means for learning; a ridiculous idea, as was quickly realised.

In theory, there is no reason why a blended solution should have to make any use of technology – a blend could easily consist of some reading from good old-fashioned books, some on-job instruction, a face-to-face workshop and a practical assignment. However, given the opportunities that the latest hardware and software provide, it is hard to imagine many blends that would not employ technology in some form.

When you learn in large chunks – let's say in something like a three-day workshop – it is quite possible to do so without exposure to much more than a few PowerPoint slides. On the other hand, when you are participating in a rich blend – making use of a wide variety of content formats, taking part in frequent live sessions, and maintaining contact with a cohort of fellow learners – it's hard not to employ technologies

such as web conferencing, discussion forums and online video.

A greater use of technology places strain on the learning professional, whose development we have sadly neglected over the past decade, as the possibilities arising from new learning media have exploded. While new, younger entrants to the profession have grown up with computers, the Internet and mobile devices, these still represent a small minority. After all, most people become involved in learning and development as a second or third career, so not many can be regarded as 'digital natives[23]'. As a result, most learners are more enthusiastic and knowledgeable about technology than their teachers and trainers, a situation that is clearly not sustainable.

A greater use of technology places strain on the learning professional, whose development we have sadly neglected over the past decade, as the possibilities arising from new learning media have exploded.

The Towards Maturity[24] benchmarking studies have shown that those organisations that have experienced the most success with learning technologies have invested in building the capability of learning professionals. Employers and education and training providers need capability in four areas: (1) the strategic management of the use of learning technologies; (2) the design of blends that make full use of available technologies; (3) the design of digital learning content; and (4) the facilitation of online learning, both live in the virtual classroom and with communities of learners working at their own pace. Learning professionals with these skills are in short supply, an incentive if ever there was one for individuals to take advantage of the opportunities to up-skill.

Introducing blended learning to an organisation is an exercise in change management. One thing we know is that

23_ This concept was first articulated by Marc Prensky in his 2001 article 'Digital Natives, Digital Immigrants'. Natives are those who have grown up with digital technologies. Immigrants are those who have adopted them later in life.

24_ Towards Maturity is a UK non-profit organisation that benchmarks the use that employers are making of learning technologies. By analysing the data from hundreds of employers over many years, they have been able to identify the characteristics of those organisations that have been most successful in applying learning technologies. See www.towardsmaturity.org.

people don't necessarily resist change – they resist being changed. We are much more likely to co-operate if we are genuinely consulted throughout the change process and our hopes and fears are taken into account. Whether we are line managers, learning professionals or learners, we want to be actively involved in shaping a future in which we can all benefit.

One thing we know is that people don't necessarily resist change – they resist being changed.

While it is important that all stakeholders can perceive the benefits of the change – essentially what's in it for them – this in itself may not be enough. Economic theory suggests that we are probably more afraid of the possibility of a loss than we are excited by the prospect of a gain.

Humans may have advanced in many ways, but something scary still gets and holds attention more quickly and for longer than something pleasant. While we could take advantage of this tendency by making clear what there is to be lost by *not* engaging with the change, this could be perceived as a form of coercion.

It is not enough to appeal to our rational brains with facts, figures and logical arguments; we have to obtain emotional buy-in. We will not achieve this by moving too fast. People can only deal with so much at once, a phenomenon that Chip and Dan Heath refer to as the 'finite pool of worry'[25].

OVERCOMING RESISTANCE TO BLENDED LEARNING

Blended learning represents, for most organisations, a significant change to the way that learning interventions are carried out. For this reason you are likely to encounter resistance, not least from managers, learners and other learning professionals.

25_ *Switch: How to change things when change is hard by Chip Heath and Dan Heath, Crown Business (2010).*

The concerns of managers

Possible concerns	How you could respond
Blended learning is likely to be more expensive than classroom training.	Far from it. The whole point of blending is to provide a more cost-effective solution than you could achieve using a single approach – otherwise you wouldn't bother!
Blended learning is likely to be more expensive than self-study e-learning.	This is possible because, once you've developed the materials, self-study is practically free to deliver. However, self-study on its own is rarely the most effective solution. By blending you get the proper balance between effectiveness and efficiency.
Blended learning will not be as effective as what we've had in the past.	Blended learning in itself is neither effective nor ineffective – it all comes down to what you put in the blend, particularly in terms of methods. Having said that, well-designed blended learning places a greater emphasis on the end-to-end learning journey than simple event-based learning, so there is a better chance of an effective end result.
It will be harder to keep track of what training our employees are supposed to be doing and when.	This is a genuine concern. Because blended learning has more elements to it, it is clearly going to be more difficult to track. For this reason, it's useful to implement blended learning in conjunction with an easy-to-use learning management solution[30.]
It will be harder to evaluate the success of the training.	Not the case. At the very least blended solutions should be no more difficult to evaluate than other approaches. At best, they can be designed to make evaluation easier than before.

Ways in which you can gain the commitment of managers:

- Consult managers when designing blended solutions, to make sure their concerns are taken into account.

- Have managers participate in blended learning courses, so they can appreciate the benefits for themselves.

- Provide managers with access to learning management tools so they can easily track the progress of their staff through the blend.

- Provide managers with figures to show how much blended learning has saved them in terms of both time and money.

30_There are now more ways to record learning activities and outcomes. As well as corporate learning management systems and virtual learning environments, the new Tin Can API (now more formally labelled the Experience API) allows for all sorts of learning – formal and informal – to be recorded in a 'Learning Record Store'. See tincanapi.com.

The concerns of learners

Possible concerns	How you could respond
I prefer training to be face to face.	Fine. Our blended solutions often include a face-to-face element, when we believe that this is necessary to achieving an effective result. But other approaches can provide some great benefits too, not least the option to work at your own pace and at a time that suits you.
I am not confident enough with computers to use them for learning.	Plenty of other employees feel like you, which is why we are providing some IT training for anyone who feels they would benefit. And when you do start using computers for learning, you'll find we've made the whole process as simple as possible.
It will be hard for me to get the time I need to meet any requirements for self-study.	You need to get the commitment of your manager to release you for the time you need to study. You may find it easier to do this work in a learning centre or at home.
It will be hard for me to keep track of what learning activities I'm supposed to be doing and when.	We've provided you with access to a learning platform which spells out clearly what the elements are in your blended solution and when they are expected to take place.
Blended learning is just a glorified cost-saving exercise.	Blended learning may save money – which is not a bad thing – but that's only half the story. We've designed our blended solutions to make sure there is no compromise on effectiveness. In some cases that means spending more!

Ways in which you can gain the commitment of learners:

- Consult learners when designing blended solutions, to make sure their concerns are taken into account.

- Make sure learners have the IT skills they need to take advantage of the technology elements in your solutions.

- Provide learners with access to learning management tools so they can easily track their progress through their courses.

- Help learners to obtain the support they need from their managers, particularly in securing the time they need to complete self-study elements of their courses.

The concerns of other learning professionals

Possible concerns	How you could respond
I don't see why we can't just carry on doing what we did in the past. No-one has complained.	In many cases we will – not all learning requirements benefit from a blended approach. In other cases, we believe we can provide efficiencies and improvements that will benefit both learners and the organisation as a whole. We cannot ignore those opportunities.
Blended learning is going to make our lives more complicated.	That's true – because blended learning obviously has more elements to it than a simple classroom or self-study approach. However, we will be taking full advantage of the features provided by our learning platform to make sure the process goes as smoothly as possible. We believe the benefits will far outweigh the small amount of extra work involved in monitoring and planning.
I'm primarily a classroom trainer. My role is going to become redundant.	Hardly. Not all of our courses will be blended and those that are will often include a classroom element. Not only that, you'll get the chance to broaden out your skills by helping us to make use of a wide range of new technologies.
I don't understand enough about blended learning to make any meaningful contribution.	Funny you should say that. There's a good book I could recommend …
How will we be able to tell whether the training's been successful?	In this respect, blended learning's really no different from anything we've done in the past. Having said that, if we make use of all the media at our disposal as well as the features provided by our learning platform, we may be able to evaluate our training more thoroughly than we've been able to before.

Ways in which you can gain the commitment of other learning professionals:

- Make sure they all get to participate in some way in either the design or the delivery of blended learning solutions.

- Provide them with access to the ideas you're reading about here, as well as the training, coaching and support they'll need, so they don't feel disadvantaged by a lack of knowledge or skills.

- Make sure all learning professionals are fully conversant with your learning management system, so they can more easily track the courses in which they are involved.

- Explain clearly what each new blended solution is going to achieve in terms of efficiencies or better learning. Share your evaluation data to help build confidence in this new approach.

ESTIMATING
THE TIME

AND COST
OF A
BLENDED SOLUTION

Blended learning is not inherently quick or inexpensive. The efficiency of a blend depends wholly on the ingredients of which it is composed.

The priority in any blend is effectiveness, which is a product of the educational and training methods that you select. As we have seen, in a blend there is likely to be a mix of social contexts for learning (learning on your own, one-to-one with an instructor, coach or facilitator, with a group of fellow learners or with a wider community) and often a number of strategies (simple exposition of information, instruction, guided discovery and exploration). These factors determine whether the blend will deliver the required learning and meet the underlying need.

There is no point in implementing a fast, inexpensive solution if it doesn't work. However, once you've locked down a methodology that will deliver the goods, you still have plenty of scope. For example, a group discussion could take place in a face-to-face workshop, a virtual classroom or on an online forum; a video could be distributed on DVD or streamed online to mobile devices; a coaching session could be conducted face to face, by telephone or on Skype.

You also have options in terms of how you resource content and expertise. Do you do all the work in-house, employ an external contractor, purchase a solution off-the-shelf, or combine these in some way? The choices you make will have a big impact on time and cost.

To determine the best way forward in each situation, you need to be able to compare each option on a directly comparable basis in terms of cost and the time required to deliver. That's not quite as simple as it may seem.

COMPARING COSTS

To compare alternative blends, you have to take account of all the costs, not just those that are directly expended on outside products and services. You would be amazed how many learning professionals only recognise direct costs, such as travel expenses, fees paid to freelance trainers or the costs of using external developers. Chances are these will represent only a small proportion of the true overall cost to your organisation.

If you only measure direct costs, you can make some bizarre decisions. I cannot remember how many times I have been told that work that is carried out in-house is free, however long it takes or inexpertly it is executed. True, internal labour is typically budgeted a long time in advance and is paid from an organisation's overhead budget, but it is certainly not free. Salaries, taxes, pensions and other benefits, not to mention all manner of support costs, are paid in hard cash by an employer, just like any direct expenditure on a training programme. If the labour was not being expended on designing, developing or delivering blended learning it could be dispensed with. Hard but true. The reality is probably that many learning professionals do not include internal costs in their calculations because they do not want to make visible just how much they cost, and you can see why.

The most important of all indirect costs is the time it takes for employees to engage in a learning solution – time that could have been spent directly contributing to the organisation's KPIs. To ignore these costs is simple madness. A blend that significantly reduces the amount of time that employees spend away from the job (assuming that the solution is at least as effective as what went before) will make a significant contribution to an organisation's profitability. In some circumstances it might be necessary to incur more direct costs to secure this time saving – let's say something like the external development of some interactive learning materials – yet the net benefit to the organisation could be substantial. If you only consider direct costs in your calculations you miss out on this potential benefit.

The following table provides a hypothetical example, looking at the first year of costs only:

	Blend 1 – a largely face-to-face solution	Blend 2 – with a reduced face-to-face element, substituted by self-study
Direct costs (in the case of blend 1, this is primarily learner travel expenses; in the case of blend 2, there is the additional cost of external development of new materials)	£10K	£30K
Indirect costs (primarily learner time away from the job; in the case of blend 2, travel time is reduced and learning time is accelerated through interactive self-study)	£100K	£50K
Total	£110K	£80K

What's more, in year two the advantage would be even greater, because the costs of the external materials would already have been absorbed. This makes the point that costs need to be viewed over an appropriate time horizon, typically the realistic lifetime of the solution.

Some elements in a blend may be expensive to develop but relatively cheap to deliver – the classic example being self-study materials. You are not going to make the right judgement if you look only at the initial period in which all the up-front costs are borne. Perhaps the most useful measure here is the cost per individual learner over the lifetime of the solution.

INVESTING NOW TO SAVE MONEY LATER

One of the greatest difficulties facing learning professionals is making comparisons between methods that have different mixes of fixed and variable costs.

Let's say you are thinking of implementing a development programme that explores important new ideas for the future running of your business. One option you have is to centre your blend on a series of face-to-face workshops for groups of, say, ten. Quite probably there are few fixed costs involved, just a modest amount of design and development time. The variable costs, on the other hand, are very high. A facilitator has to be present at each workshop and all participants have to travel to the events.

In contrast, you could decide to run your programme as a large-scale online course, with unlimited numbers of participants. Let's say you decide to invest a considerable amount of time and effort in producing videos and interactive scenarios to provide a catalyst for assignments and online discussions that pretty well run by themselves. The fixed costs are relatively high.

If only a handful of people take the course, the costs would be much higher than the equivalent face-to-face offering. However, what if 100 enrol, or 1,000, or 10,000[26]? The incremental delivery cost for each new learner becomes closer and closer to zero (although, as we've already seen, the learner's time is also a critical element).

	Option 1 – the blend centres on face-to-face workshops	Option 2 – large-scale online programme
Development cost	£5,000	£50,000
Delivery cost per learner (time away from work)	£500	£500
Facilitator costs per learner	£200	£50
Cost per learner if 10 people take the course	£1,200	£5,550
Cost per learner if 1,000 take the course	£700	£600
Cost per learner if 10,000 take the course	£700	£555

26_ The advent of MOOCs (Massive Open Online Courses) makes even these figures seem like an underestimate. Popular MOOCs can easily attract many tens of thousands of students, perhaps in the future millions.

TIME MATTERS TOO

As the example above shows, the more learners enrol on the programme, the greater the advantage of investing the £50,000 in the development of new materials (the fixed costs), as delivery costs drop because of the reduced need for facilitation (the variable costs). If you were to set aside the £500 cost of the learner's time (as you could do if you were calculating costs from the point of view of an educational or training provider such as a college, as opposed to an employer), the difference would be much more obvious.

But the cost of designing, developing and delivering a learning solution is not the only consideration when choosing a blend. In many cases, time is every bit as important, both timeliness (the training occurs at an appropriate time – neither too early or too late) and time to competence.

There is a real cost to an organisation of an employee not being fully competent to do their job; a cost that keeps racking up day after day. So, while cost per learner may be a useful measure, alongside this we also have to consider how long it would take to deliver the solution to the entire target population.

There is a real cost to an organisation of an employee not being fully competent to do their job; a cost that keeps racking up day after day.

Going back to our previous example, if there was a requirement to train 10,000 employees, then you would be seriously held back by the need to find enough facilitators to run all those workshops for groups of ten at a time. Let's face it, there simply is no way you can run 1,000 workshops quickly. But you *can* run one very large-scale online programme. And that's where timeliness comes into the equation.

Getting the job done quickly means that there are less people in the organisation without the skills needed to do their job properly or, to put it more positively, more people out there doing the best they can.

IN CONCLUSION

So, we've seen that, while our first priority is to come up with an effective blend, we need a systematic way of comparing all the different ways we could implement that blend. That means taking all costs into account, not just those that require an external payment. It also means taking a longer-term view over the lifetime of a solution, and looking for approaches that get the job done sooner rather than later.

IMPLEM

ENTING
YOUR
BLENDS

MARKET YOUR PROGRAMME

Blended learning solutions have to be sold, just like any other product or service. This is particularly important when many learners and their managers have had little or no experience of blended learning and may be apprehensive about its benefits. Marketing is important even when the programme is compulsory, as you want employees to participate in your courses in the right frame of mind – not grudgingly.

Here are some ways in which you can encourage take-up:

- Make senior management aware of the programme you are intending to run and any benefits it will provide in terms of increases in volume, reductions in costs, the speed with which people become competent performers, and overall quality.

- Involve learners and managers in the design and development of your programme. These people will become your champions.

- Use your organisation's news media (your intranet, e-newsletters, house magazines, etc.) to announce the programme. Provide a steady stream of news about the programme to keep the story alive.

- Provide briefing sessions for managers and/or potential participants.

- Make sure potential learners are fully aware of the benefits that the programme could provide for them in terms of job satisfaction, career progression or job security.

- Celebrate when employees gain new skills, complete their courses and gain qualifications. Celebrate when departments experience performance improvements as a result of their learning. Interview satisfied learners and managers to provide material for yet more news stories.

- Publish statistics on course completions. Reinforce these statistics with estimates of cost savings and other tangible benefits.

Involve learners and managers in the design and development of your programme. These people will become your champions.

KEEP THE PROGRAMME ON TRACK

Ideally you want participants to complete your blended learning courses, obtain the certifications or qualifications that are associated with these, move forward with increased competence and confidence, and enjoy the experience. This requires that you put the right policies in place and then manage the courses carefully when they are in progress.

Tracking progress

Here are some ways in which you can keep track of progress:

Use your learning platform: Make use of the information provided by your LMS (learning management system) or VLE (virtual learning environment) to keep you in touch with the numbers participating in your programme, the progress they are making through the various elements of the blend and completions. It has long been possible to keep track of e-learning completions and scores using specifications such as SCORM[27], but the new Experience API (often called 'Tin Can') now makes it possible to also keep track of more informal and offline experiences. Even without SCORM or Tin Can, many LMSs and VLEs allow learners to check off activities as they are completed.

27_ SCORM is the Sharable Content Object Reference Model, a set of standards, specifications and guidelines to allow interoperability between learning management systems and learning content. See www.adlnet. gov/scorm/.

Meet with managers: If you are finding that take-up, student progress or completions are not on target, meet with managers and team leaders to find out what obstacles there may be and act to remove them.

Build in progress reviews: Make sure your courses contain regular reviews, which allow participants to communicate any difficulties they are experiencing.

Provide proactive tutoring: If your courses provide for tutorial support, make sure that tutors take the initiative to resolve problems rather than wait to be asked.

Encouraging completion

It is not always important that learners complete courses – after all, if learners have got what they are after, there is really no point in them simply going through the motions and sticking it out right to the end. However, there will be situations when a learner who does not complete a course becomes a disillusioned learner and will be reluctant to embark on a similar programme in the future. Here are some strategies you can employ to encourage learners to fully participate in a course and go on to complete what they have started:

> It is not always important that learners complete courses – after all, if learners have got what they are after, there is really no point in them simply going through the motions and sticking it out right to the end.

Make the programme compulsory: This won't guarantee completion, but it will help. On the other hand, it could just cause resentment, which is not the ideal starting point for a programme.

Make a charge: Typically you assign less value to something that is free. If you pay for a course (or your department or employer does) then there is a stronger incentive to receive a return on that investment.

Agree responsibilities: Sometimes it is not clear to learners what the implications are for not participating in activities, particularly those that involve other students. Encourage learners to agree up front that they have responsibilities, to their facilitator, to their manager, to their fellow students and, most of all, to themselves.

Some organisations have learners and their managers sign contracts before embarking on a major development programme: the learner agrees to put in the time and keep up with the programme; the manager agrees to provide whatever support is necessary, including the time necessary for the learner to participate fully.

Make your application exercises relevant: Learners will be less motivated to undertake assignments that they don't see as relevant to their real work. Try to devise activities that combine real work with the application of new skills and ideas.

Provide incentives: The best incentive is probably a portable qualification that you can put on your CV. If not, perhaps the course will improve the learner's career prospects within the organisation. Whatever happens, if the course is directly relevant to the learner's work, it will help them to attain mastery in their job, something for which we all strive.

Set deadlines: Courses with milestones and finish dates have far lower dropout rates.

Use peer pressure: Courses that learners start and finish as a group have higher completion rates, because no learner wants to be left behind. You might want to publish tables which show who has completed which activities.

Provide recognition: Celebrate all successes publicly.

LOOK AHEAD TO MINIMISE PROBLEMS

A major new blended learning programme is an exciting prospect, but not without risks. However thoroughly you have considered your implementation plan, it makes sense to double check where potential problems might lie and take whatever precautionary steps are necessary to avoid these occurring or to minimise their effects.

The pre-mortem

Gary Klein introduced the idea of a pre-mortem. When you have almost come to an important decision, but not formally committed yourself, you gather together key people who are knowledgeable about the decision. The premise of the session is to imagine that you are a year into the future. You have implemented the plan as it now exists and the outcome was a disaster. You take 10 minutes to write a brief history of that disaster.

The pre-mortem will force you to envisage the worst things that could happen to scupper your plans. You then have two choices: (1) reconsider your decision, or (2) take steps to reduce the risks of the disaster happening.

The pre-mortem will force you to envisage the worst things that could happen to scupper your plans.

Potential problem analysis

One way to ensure you think through each major risk thoroughly is to conduct a potential problem analysis:

1. Identify a potential problem that is both serious and possible (in other words it is not a chance in a million!).

2. Consider what could cause this problem to occur.

3. Identify what you could do to remove this cause, i.e. to stop the problem occurring in the first place. This will not always be entirely possible, so continue to step 4.

4. Consider what would be the most likely effect of this problem occurring.

5. Identify what you could do to minimise this effect should the problem occur.

6. You can extend the analysis by looking at additional probable causes and effects.

Here is an example of an analysis of the potential problem of students failing to complete self-study assignments:

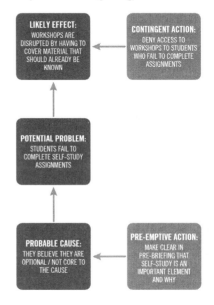

MEASURING
SUCCESS

You cannot manage what you do not measure. You owe it to all your stakeholders – project sponsors, managers, learning professionals and learners – to check whether a blended programme has contributed to meeting the need on which the original design was based, whether it has delivered value for money, and whether it can be improved for the future.

You cannot manage what you do not measure.

Your goal from the onset has been to deliver an effective solution as efficiently and flexibly as you can. Let's start with some ideas for ways in which you can measure effectiveness.

EFFECTIVENESS

How did learners react to the programme?

This level of evaluation is extremely commonplace; it is also more often than not the only form of evaluation that does take place. The measurement of reactions is much derided because it is seen to deliver only superficial information – 'The trainer was very knowledgeable', 'The lunch was scrumptious' – but in my mind it remains an essential component. What business does not want to know how its customers respond to its products and services? What business would not be alarmed if the reaction was hostile? After all, complaints spread from peer to peer all too easily, and before long you have no customers at all.

There are several ways of assessing the reactions of learners to their blended learning experience:

- Having learners complete evaluation forms at the completion of the course and/or (ideally, if you want reflective responses) some time after. These could be paper-based or completed online.

- Asking trainers and facilitators to record their own observations on how well the course has gone.

- Holding review meetings during and/or after the course. These could be face-to-face, online or by teleconference.

- Using a discussion forum to record learners' thoughts and suggestions.

- Having learners complete a journal in the form of a blog in which they record their feelings as they progress through a course.

It is important to ask the right questions. Ideally you want specific information about the learner's reactions to particular resources and activities, so you can make whatever adjustments are necessary. You want to know how long particular activities took, so you can revise your estimates. You want to know how relevant the content was, what frustrations the learner felt, what they enjoyed and what they found rewarding. Or you could borrow from the marketing profession and ask what Fred Reichheld calls the ultimate question: 'How likely is it that you would recommend us to a friend?'

What learning took place?

Learning (the acquisition of new knowledge, skills and ideas) is not normally the final outcome of a blend that follows the PIAF process, but it is an important step along the way. The techniques that you choose to assess learning will obviously depend on the type of learning you are looking to achieve and the media you have chosen for your blend. Here are some suggestions:

- E-assessments, graded automatically by the system.

- Essays completed on paper or online.

- Projects and assignments submitted and assessed. Most learning management platforms provide facilities for project work to be uploaded and then assessed by peers and/or tutors.

- Simulations, whether live or computer-based.

- Observed practical exercises, such as role-plays.

- Learner contributions to discussion forums and other social media.

- Portfolios (and increasingly e-portfolio systems) that collect together evidence of learning from a range of activities.

- Self-assessments.

How did the learner's behaviour change?
Learning in itself is of little value if it is not applied to real-life situations. Here are some ways to measure behaviour change:

- Questionnaires completed by managers, peers and subordinates, probably online.

- Self-reporting by learners themselves.

- Observation by trainers, coaches, etc.

- Activity monitoring software.

- The learner maintains a journal in the form of a blog in the weeks following

a course, describing their experiences in applying what they have learned.

- Competence assessments by managers, based on observation or portfolios of evidence.

Did the changes in behaviour impact on the organisation's performance?
Ultimately, you'll want to know whether your blended solution has addressed the need on which it was based. Performance improvement can be reported by managers and learners or objectively measured using key performance indicators such as the numbers of complaints, employee turnover, sales made, output per hour and so on.

To show the improvement, you will have to measure both before and after your programme. For absolute reliability (and this is probably only going to be worthwhile for very large programmes or those that represent a major new investment) you should compare the results of learners with those of a control group that has not gone through the programme.

EFFICIENCY

Efficiency can also be measured in a wide range of ways:

Cost against budget: Did the programme come in on budget?

Cost per student: How much did it cost for a single student to participate in the programme, taking account of all factors, including time away from the job?

Comparative cost: Did the programme cost less than it might have done previously, assuming it used a different approach?

Duration: How much time did it take for a student to complete the programme? Was this more or less than before you used a blended approach?

Timeliness: Was the programme delivered at the right time to meet the needs of the organisation and/or the individual learners?

Time to competence: How long does it take for a person to become a competent performer?

Throughput: How many people in total were you able to train in a given period?

Reach: Was the programme accessible to a wider audience than was previously possible?

Usage of capacity: Were resources wasted in the design, development and delivery of the programme? For example, were group sizes lower than anticipated? Were external resources used when internal skills were available?

BRINGING IT ALL TOGETHER

There are various ways in which you can bring together measures of effectiveness and efficiency. Ultimately you are looking to answer the question 'was all this effort worthwhile?'

Return on investment
Return on investment (ROI) is a measure of the extent to which the performance outputs of a programme, expressed in financial terms, exceeded the inputs to the programme (essentially the costs).

ROI is calculated for a specific period of time, typically a year, but sometimes longer if the programme has an extended lifetime or if it is unrealistic to expect quick returns. The calculation is made quite simply as follows:

$$ROI\% = \frac{financial\ return - cost}{cost} \times 100$$

For example, if you invested £10K in a programme and received a return of £12K, the ROI would be £12K - £10K = £2K / £10K = 20%.

As we saw in the chapter on estimating time and cost, it is important to include both direct and indirect costs in your calculation. If you only include the direct elements (where an external payment is made) you could be missing more than 80% of the cost, much of which will be the expense of lost student time.

Performance outputs can be difficult to measure in financial terms but, in the absence of hard data, your best estimates are a lot better than nothing.

Cost-benefit analysis
Cost-benefit analysis (CBA) was introduced in the 1930s and is commonly used to compare alternative options. CBA is similar to ROI in that it compares financial returns and costs over a given time period. The difference is that you do not get to express the difference between the two as a percentage.

Return on expectation
ROI or cost-benefit analysis may seem like the ultimate measure of achievement but many argue that it is up to the stakeholders in a learning intervention to determine how success should be measured. What we are looking at is the extent to which we have fulfilled the expectations of our 'business partners' – those who first expressed the need on which our intervention was founded. This may have been expressed financially, but in many cases not. The expectation may have been for increased sales or reduced waste, but it could as easily have been for an improvement in morale or commitment to a new set of values.

The terms of a Return on Expectation (ROE) are agreed before a project begins, bringing stakeholders together in the effort to define and measure a meaningful target. In contrast, ROI is typically calculated in hindsight and in terms that may not be useful to key stakeholders.

And so we come full circle. We started with a need and we ended by evaluating our success in meeting that need. But because this is a circle, our work is not done. We will be looking to constantly refine and improve our blend until the need is completely satisfied. That way we have no regrets.

10

TEN TIPS FOR BETTER BLENDS

There is nothing inherently wonderful about a blended solution. Making the decision to design an intervention in a blended format is only your first step – the quality of your end result depends on what you include in the blend and when, and how well these decisions reflect the learning requirement, the characteristics of your target population and the particular resource constraints within which you are being asked to operate.

The following tips will not guarantee you will make great design decisions but they may just point you in the right direction.

ANALYSING THE SITUATION

Tip 1: Don't jump to solutions – start with a sound analysis

This one's a bit obvious, but it needs saying. It's oh so tempting when confronted with a new project to jump straight into the creative process of selecting the ingredients for your blend without a clear understanding of what it is that you're required to achieve. There will be plenty of room for creativity later on in the design process, although you may find that the 'how' becomes all too obvious once you have answered the questions 'what', 'why', 'who for', 'by when' and 'for how much'.

To conduct a thorough analysis you need to be systematic and persistent; systematic to make sure you fully explore all aspects of the learning, the learners and the logistics, and persistent, because project sponsors may be reluctant to answer so many questions. A good test is how clearly you feel you could articulate the requirement to a third party; if you cannot explain it properly, then you don't understand it well enough.

Tip 2: Try to stop the subject expert and the client dictating the solution

A subject-matter expert should be your friend and partner, but he or she should not be your master. His or her role is to ensure the quality of the technical content; yours is to ensure that the learning objectives are achieved. Of course the SME may be able to provide you with valuable insights into the best ways to communicate their expertise, but they are not ideally placed to offer this advice. Why? Because subject experts suffer from 'the curse of knowledge[28]' – they believe that every aspect of their subject is not only of vital importance but intrinsically

interesting to just about anyone. They are wrong.

A subject-matter expert should be your friend and partner, but he or she should not be your master.

The situation is similar with clients and other forms of project sponsor. Try not to let them dictate to you how their needs should be met. Your relationship should be one of professional adviser, not order taker. The client's responsibility is to articulate their needs. Yours is to help them to meet these needs effectively and efficiently.

Tip 3: Focus on performance, not knowledge

Schools and colleges exist primarily to foster learning. Employers are really only interested in learning to the extent that it influences performance. They invest in learning interventions because they believe these will positively impact on their key performance indicators, but they have lots of other ways to spend their money and need reassurance that they are getting a good return.

28_ *The idea of the curse of knowledge was first expressed by Chip and Dan Heath in their book Made to Stick, Random House (2007).*

> Employers are really only interested in learning to the extent that it influences performance.

So, focus in on business needs and what employees need to be doing differently or better if these needs are to be met. Then ask yourself what employees absolutely *must* know if they are to do the things that the business needs. This focus will ensure you don't overload employees with information they don't need and that, instead, you provide lots of opportunities for them to practise and build confidence.

DETERMINING METHODS

Tip 4: Don't overdo the self-study

Self-study provides attractive benefits to learners, particularly in the control that it allows them over what they learn, when, where and at what pace. It also puts a smile on the face of the finance director, because it's so cheap, at least when there are lots of people who require training. But blends have to be effective as well as cheap and flexible. As we've seen, they must deliver in terms of performance.

Self-study works well in small doses, but we are social animals and we need to externalise our learning, to reassure ourselves of our progress, and to compare our thoughts with others. Not only that; after prolonged periods of self-study we are going to be bursting with questions and comments that can only be adequately resolved by contact with coaches, experts and peers.

Tip 5: Build in lots of opportunities to practise new skills

We have already discussed how easy it is to overload learners with information, particularly abstract theory, facts and procedures. Another side effect of our focus on knowledge is that we allow far too little time for learners to practise new skills. Imagine if you went to a tennis lesson and spent the whole time watching videos and discussing tactics: how frustrating would this be?

Generally speaking it's best to provide the learner with the absolute minimum amount of information they need before they can start practising. You can top up on the theory later, as they encounter difficulties and are striving to get better. That's why coaching can play a valuable role in so many blends.

Tip 6: Use guided discovery to get across the big ideas

Some tasks are rule-based – they are carried out in accordance with clearly laid-down policies and procedures. But nearly all jobs also require the incumbent to make at least some judgements in highly variable situations. These tasks are principle-based; they rely on the employee's ability to make sense of the myriad of cause and effect relationships that impact on them in their work.

It is rarely effective to convey principles through exposition or instruction. You will not be nicer to customers, stop eating chocolate or finish your meetings on time just because someone else tells you these things are important. You need to discover the big ideas for yourself, either through hard experience, by observing others or through a learning activity that has been designed specially to encourage those 'aha' moments.

You need to discover the big ideas for yourself, either through hard experience, by observing others or through a learning activity that has been designed specially to encourage those 'aha' moments.

SELECTING MEDIA

Tip 7: Keep a balance between the synchronous and asynchronous

Asynchronous (same-time) media work at your pace – there is no requirement for you to be 'in sync' with anyone else. You can consume the contents of books, DVDs and iPods – or their online equivalents – whenever you want; you have similar flexibility when you communicate using email, forums, SMS and social networks.

But there's something special about participating in a live event in the company of your peers. It focuses your energies and helps to ensure you keep up-to-date with your self-paced learning activities. Synchronous (own-time) experiences, whether face-to-face, online or on the telephone, enrich a blend and provide it with momentum. Sometimes a blend can be too flexible – it makes it too easy to put off those essential learning tasks until another day.

Tip 8: Keep all ideas about technology out of your mind until you've fixed on a suitable method

Technology will rarely make much of an impact on the effectiveness of your solution. Yes it could make it faster, cheaper, more flexible and more scalable, but it won't guarantee that you achieve your goals. The first priority in any learning design – once you have a clear understanding of the requirement – is to establish the strategies that will best facilitate the required learning for your particular population.

Once you have a strategy that you believe in, don't compromise. There is absolutely no point in going for a highly efficient solution that doesn't work. So, take each element in your strategy and ask yourself how you can deliver this efficiently and flexibly, without compromising on the intended outcomes. Technology is a tool, not a goal in itself.

Tip 9: Recognise that face-to-face learning still has an important part to play

However fast your bandwidth and however high-resolution your webcam, you cannot fully replicate a multi-sensory, face-to-face experience online – at least not for now. There are occasions when learners really do need to get hands-on with tools and equipment (perhaps even with each other), explore a real physical space, tune in to the body language of others in the room or just experience the magic of the occasion.

Most learning does not require you to be face to face with others – just like you happily listen to music on your iPod, watch sport on TV or films at the cinema – but some does. While face-to-face learning will increasingly become the special case rather than the default, it is likely to still have a valuable role to play. Imagine if you never, ever got to go to a theatre, watch a live band or join the crowd at a football stadium.

Imagine if you never, ever got to go to a theatre, watch a live band or join the crowd at a football stadium.

THE OVERALL PROCESS

Tip 10: Extend the blend along the whole learning journey

For far too long we have deluded ourselves into thinking that we can achieve meaningful learning through a single live event or using a single resource, however brilliantly these are facilitated or designed. Learning is a process, a journey, which takes time and a wide range of initiatives, some by teachers, trainers and coaches, but many by learners themselves.

One of the primary arguments for blending is that it allows us to dispense with the idea of learning as an event and to look at providing just the right support to the learner at every step they take from ignorance to mastery. This starts by helping them prepare for the journey they will be taking, providing formal learning activities and resources, encouraging application to the real work situation, and then following-up as long as needed with additional input and guidance. That's further than most learning departments currently go, but anything less is a job half done, at best.

a

THE

BL

COLLECTION:

PwC

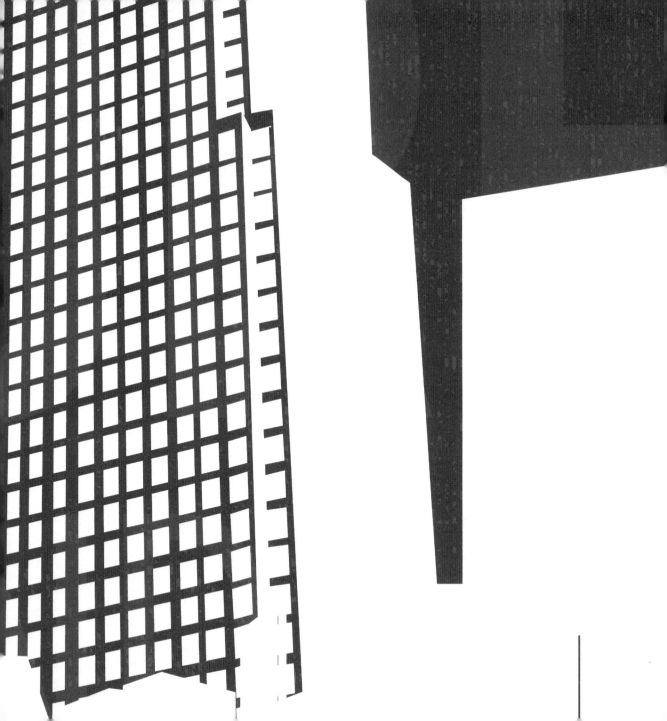

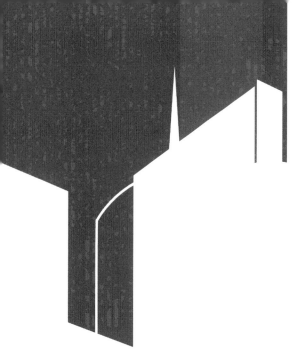

PWC: LEARNING IN THE BRAND STYLE

This case study demonstrates how a rich blend of different approaches can be needed to practically implement a major change across a large, international organisation. Particularly interesting is the wide range of resources that PwC used to embed the change and support employees long after the formal element of the blend had been completed.

TALKING ABOUT THE BRAND CURRICULUM

Sarah Lindsell, Director, Global Learning Technology, PwC

The business need that gave rise to the project was the rebrand of PwC, which took place a couple of years ago. It's a five-year programme that changes not only the way we look, but also the way we think, write and speak. Our market analysis showed that we needed to communicate differently with our clients. We needed to speak more plainly and make every single one of our words count.

The brand curriculum is made up of five core elements. The first and simplest provides training on the new brand PowerPoint templates, along with tips and techniques. The second uses a simulation-based approach to communicate the power brand-awareness has on us all. The third is specifically how you write in the new brand style. The fourth is about writing reports and the fifth developing proposals.

The curriculum isn't just about explaining to our people about the new brand colours and why we are changing. We needed to change their attitudes towards branding and communication as well as give them the skills to write and communicate differently. We had to cover the whole spectrum of learning.

The audience for the programme is huge. It touches absolutely everybody in PwC, and today that stands at nearly 200,000 people. That's from an executive assistant who is creating a PowerPoint presentation, through to a partner who is in charge of a client account. It couldn't be a one size fits all curriculum.

In addition to our existing population, the curriculum needed to address our new joiners. We have a large graduate recruitment programme and, combined with our experienced hire population, we on-board thousands of new joiners to the firm each year. Some of these people may have limited exposure to what PwC is, what it stands for, or how it goes about its business. The curriculum had to be really informative for them, but also change the behaviours of skilled and experienced people who had been here for years.

Keith Resseau,
Global Digital Learning, PwC

From the start, information about the training was built in to the communications that accompanied the new brand initiative. We provided a grid explaining the different training options available.

We had to reach everyone in the network. And, depending on where you were, that meant the training had to look a little bit different. Some territories had a strong preference for doing something face to face, but we knew that couldn't be sustained everywhere.

In some places like territories with a widely dispersed population, virtual classroom made sense. For other components of the programme, we knew it would be very important to get a consistent message out and that pointed us towards e-learning.

The initial rollout was a massive effort. However, now that's completed, some of the e-learns are built in to our onboarding experience. New employees are also directed out to Spark, our social media and collaboration site, for the job aids, quick reference cards, proposal writing guides and the other things that support the formal element of the training. The e-learnings we created are popular and have won industry awards.

Writing is not a skill you would normally think to teach via e-learning. We had to think very cleverly about how to embed practice activities in a meaningful way. One of the things we did was a cut-and-paste activity. Learners had to identify the lead idea or topic for a piece of writing – which sometimes is buried several paragraphs down. They find it, select it and move it to the top. Another activity was to go through actual writing samples and choose the best replacements for jargon.

Once learners completed the training, we knew there would be a need for reinforcement back on the job. We accomplished that in a few ways.

Spark was a wonderful tool for us. We were able to provide quick access to job aids, quick reference cards and proposal writing guides. We even have a really interesting Spark thread, where people log the jargon that they hear on the job and challenge others to replace it.

Another really helpful thing is the PowerPoint templates built into everyone's desktop. It's a suite of tools that include charts, artwork, templates, page layouts and fonts. We built a short e-learn that shows people how to use this add-in. We're giving people the tools right there on their desktop when they're building presentations to include all these elements and do the job properly.

Another element of the blend is the ability to take a proposal that you're working on and send it off to a help desk. You can get feedback from someone who is an expert in our brand style to provide feedback, before you send it to a client. At a territory level, we offer clinics. An expert in your territory can come in and work with your team on the best practices of the brand style as you work on actual proposals.

Sarah

The programme overall has been a phenomenal success. One hundred per cent of people who completed the e-learns said that they were effective, and they would use the skills and knowledge that they've learnt back on the job.

We also have evidence that our clients think it's been successful and changed the way we interact with them.

But I think it's been a game changer from an L&E standpoint. This project was a successful example of a blended approach, and its success was pivotal to convincing people to do things differently.

We've had a lot of people come back to us to look at how we designed the programme, and how they can apply the same principles with new initiatives in PwC. I'm personally really proud that we took centre stage in this programme.

ANALYSED: PWC'S BRAND CURRICULUM

The situation

The need	The programme responded to a major re-branding exercise, which went well beyond the logo and colours to change the view of PwC's 200,000 globally-dispersed staff across their network of firms both of their brand and how they communicate with clients.
The learning	Apart from the need to communicate the key elements of the new branding, PwC needed to shift attitudes, build communication skills and write naturally and with a purpose.
The learners	The programme had to reach every one of PwC's 200,000 employees, from new joiners to long-serving executives.
The logistics	Sheer numbers meant that the approach had to be scalable. It also had to be flexible enough to cope with different needs, preferences and circumstances and work across different cultures in multiple countries.

ANALYSED: PWC'S BRAND CURRICULUM

The blend

	Methods	*Media*
Preparation	The training programme was introduced along with the communications that accompanied the re-branding.	Online
	New employees are automatically assigned modules from the curriculum depending on their role.	
		Using the learning management system
Input	Workshops	Either face to face or using virtual classrooms
	Self-study modules	E-learns ranging from the quite simple to mobile simulations
Application	A variety of practical exercises were built in to the self-study materials	Online
	Real world practice	Proposal-writing clinics
Follow-up	Job aids, quick reference cards and proposal-writing guides.	Accessed through Spark, the social media and collaboration site
	Discussions	Forums within Spark
	PowerPoint performance support tools	Tools and templates built in to PowerPoint
	Proposal writing support	Online help desk and face-to-face clinics

ABOUT THE AUTHOR

Clive Shepherd

Clive is a specialist in workplace learning and development, with a particular interest in the opportunities provided by new learning media. In a career spanning more than 35 years, Clive has headed up a corporate training function, co-founded a leading multimedia development business and operated as an independent consultant operating worldwide.

In recent years Clive has devoted his attention to the design and implementation of next generation blended learning solutions. He is a regular speaker at international conferences, has been recognised with two lifetime achievement awards, has written numerous books and hundreds of articles, and contributes regularly to his blog, Clive on Learning. For four years he was Chair of the eLearning Network.

Follow Clive:

Twitter:
http://www.twitter.com/cliveshepherd

Clive on Learning:
http://clive-shepherd.blogspot.com

LinkedIn:
http://uk.linkedin.com/in/cliveshepherd

Printed in Great Britain
by Amazon

81143556R00157